A Grammatical Study of Lunyankole-Lukiga

A Grammatical Study of Lunyankole-Lukiga

Edward Nobel Bisamunyu

Copyright © 2011 by Edward Nobel Bisamunyu.

ISBN: Softcover   978-1-4568-6804-8
          Ebook   978-1-4568-6805-5

All rights reserved. No part of this book may be reproduced or transmitted in any form or by any means, electronic or mechanical, including photocopying, recording, or by any information storage and retrieval system, without permission in writing from the copyright owner.

This book was printed in the United States of America.

To order additional copies of this book, contact:
Xlibris Corporation
0-800-644-6988
www.xlibrispublishing.co.uk
Orders@xlibrispublishing.co.uk
301551

CONTENTS

Introduction 9
Author's Note 17

Chapter One - Our Vowels and Consonants/
   Engambisa N'engambisibwa.................................... 21
Chapter Two - Our Greetings and Farewells/
   Endamukanya N'ensibuurana 24
Chapter Three - Our Numbers and Ordinals/
   Okubara Nokubarwa 33
Chapter Four - The Lunar Calendar/Okweezi Kumwe 39
Chapter Five - Telling The Time/Eshaaha Zeitu 47
Chapter Six - Our Personal Pronouns Ebikubyo Byeitu 54
Chapter Seven - Our Verbs Enkora 59
Chapter Eight - Affirmative and Negative/
   Obubaho N'obutabaho 69
Chapter Nine - Conjugating Verbs Okugeita Enkora 75
Chapter Ten - Reflexive Infinitive Verbs/
   Enkora Ezegarukiremu 79
Chapter Eleven - The People (Omu-Aba) Group/
   Omugabo gwabaantu (Omu-Aba) 83
Chapter Twelve - The Eki-Ebi Noun Group/
   Omugabo gwa Eki-Ebi 89
Chapter Thirteen - The E-Ama Noun Group/
   Omugabo gwa E-Ama 92
Chapter Fourteen - The Omu-Emi Noun Group/
   Omugabo gwa Omu-Emi 97

Chapter Fifteen - THE OKU-AMA NOUN GROUP/
OMUGABO GWA OKU-AMA.. 102

Chapter Sixteen - THE EM-EM/EN-EN NOUN GROUP/
OMUGABO GWA EM-EM/EN-EN 105

Chapter Seventeen - THE MISCELLANEOUS NOUNS/
EMIGABO EYEMIRINGO 110

Chapter Eighteen - THE IMPORTED NOUNS/
AMAZIINA GAHEERU 113

Chapter Nineteen - PARTS OF THE HUMAN BODY/
EBICHWEEKA BYOMUBIRI 118

Chapter Twenty - OUR TENSES OBWIIRE 121

Chapter Twenty-One - THE FUTURE TENSE EBIRYAKORWA 124

Chapter Twenty-Two - THE SIMPLE PRESENT EBIRIKUKORWA......... 128

Chapter Twenty-Three - THE PRESENT CONTINUOUS TENSE/
EBIKWEISE NIBIKORWA 130

Chapter Twenty-Four - THE PAST PARTICIPLE EBYAMARWA 136

Chapter Twenty-Five - THE PAST TENSE EBYAMAZIRWE................ 139

Chapter Twenty-Six - PREPOSITIONS EMYAANYA 141

Chapter Twenty-Seven - THE IMPERATIVE VERB/
ENDAGYIRIRO 142

Chapter Twenty-Eight - CONDITIONAL TENSES/
KURI NOGYIRA.. 145

Chapter Twenty-Nine - POSSESSIVE PRONOUNS/
BITUUNGW'OHA?... 153

Chapter Thirty - RELATIVE PRONOUNS ENYOREKYERERO............. 158

Chapter Thirty-One - OUR ADJECTIVES ENSHOBOOROZI 160

Chapter Thirty-Two - OUR ADVERBS EMITWARIZE 166

Chapter Thirty-Three - OUR RELATIONSHIPS/
ABANYABUZAARE 174

Chapter Thirty-Four - SUBJECT & OBJECT PRONOUNS/
AMAZIINA GA BYOONA 176

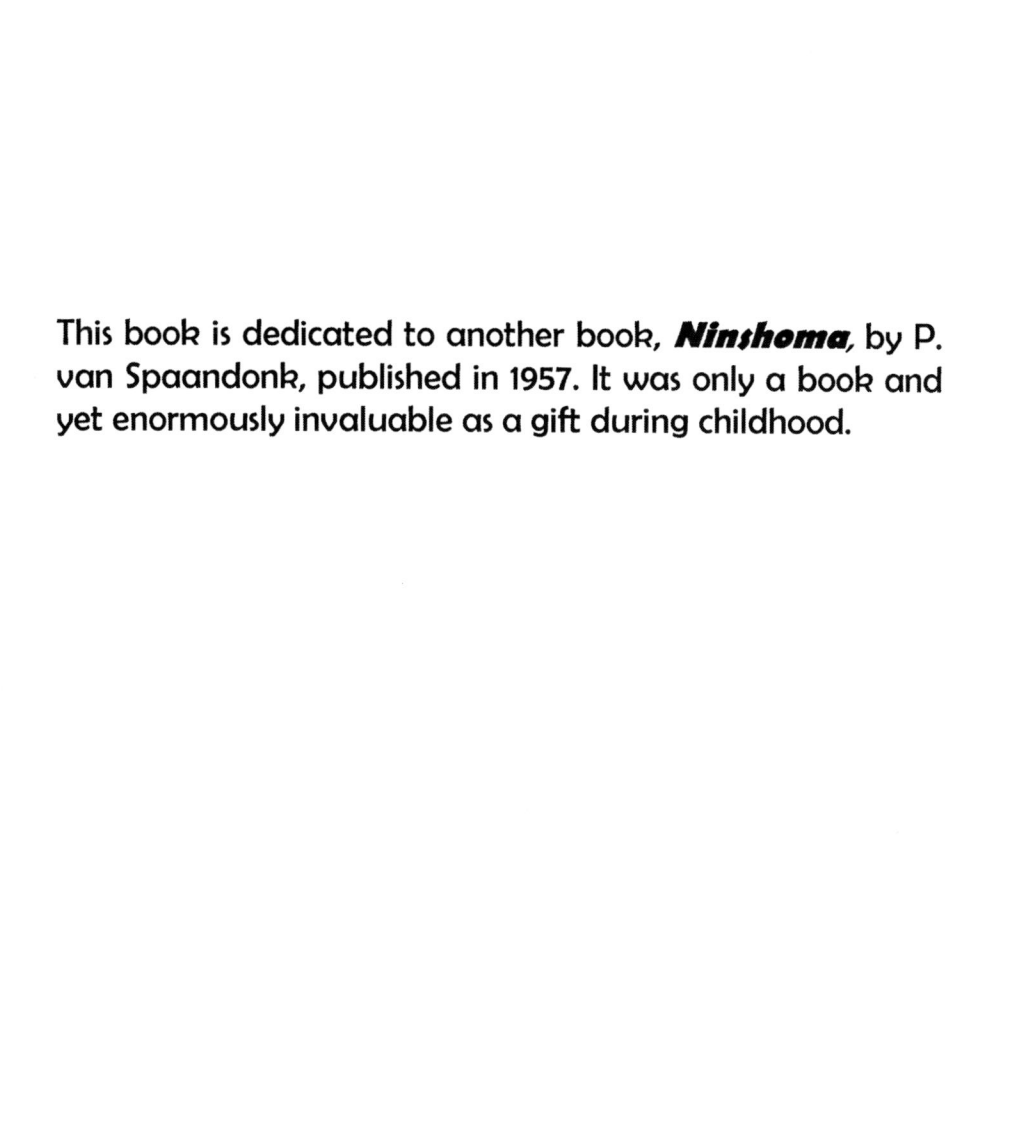

This book is dedicated to another book, **Ninshoma**, by P. van Spaandonk, published in 1957. It was only a book and yet enormously invaluable as a gift during childhood.

Introduction

PHOTO BY EDWARD NOBEL BISAMUNYU

ABAANA B'ABAKIGA NIBAKISOOMA AHARI KENGOMA PRIMARY SCHOOL, KABALE
BAKIGA PUPILS DANCING AT KENGOMA PRIMARY SCHOOL, KABALE

LUKIGA AND LUNYANKOLE-A USEFUL INTRODUCTION

African languages fall into several linguistic groups one of which, the Bantu, includes many languages found in Uganda, Kenya, Tanzania and many other countries south of the Sahara. The various Bantu languages have the word for person as a variation on one theme: **-muntu.**[1] For some languages this is a complete word and for others it is a root word to which an article prefix is appended. The variations on the theme include **omuntu** in Lunyankole-Lukiga, the prevalent languages in Kigezi and Ankole and **umuntu** in Lunyarwanda, the dominant language in Rwanda, just across the border from that part of South West Uganda that includes Kigezi and Ankole.

In the plural form, Lunyankole-Lukiga refers to people as **abantu** while Rwandese, or Rwandan, deploys a similar word, pronounced **abaannu.** Luganda, a language in southern Uganda, has **bantu,** which seems to have lost the **a-**prefix beforehand along the way or never gained one. Given that the Baganda have their origins in the more ancient Kingdom of Bunyoro, the absence of this **a-**prefix shows that a historical linguistic change may have occurred.

Bakiga of Kigezi and Banyankole of Ankole are part of the Bantu linguistic group. The root **-ntu,** which infers a person or people as well as a thing[2] and things depending on the prefix that is used with it, is common to all Bantu languages, hence their name. Note, however, that Bantu languages can be as closely related as British English is to Australian English but also as divergent from one another as Swedish is to French. A Japanese person, for example, would be called **Omujapaani.** The plural for the Japanese is **Abajapaani.** So, Bakiga refer to their name as Abakiga while Baganda drop the prefix **A-**in this name and refer to them as Bakiga.[3]

---

[1] It's interesting that a thing, or things, also have the root-ntu in their name! We differentiate them from people by giving them diminutive prefixes: **akaantu/obuntu, ekintu/ebintu,** etc.

[2] A thing or things are best seen as appliances or tools that can be put to use by a person or people. The usage of this suffix or root **-ntu** probably derived from the fact that things as tools were an important part of life. In Lunyankole-Lukiga, we indicate the difference between a human or humans and a thing or things by placing specific prefixes before the **-ntu** root. I shall explain this in detail in the following pages.

[3] Even though we have no convention for the use of capital letters in writing in Lukiga, the British English conventions that we follow generally dictate that we use capital letters for names.

The language of Baganda, or Abaganda, as they are known to Banyankole and Bakiga, dominates current literature so that most names of cultural groups in Uganda are written in Luganda. Languages, therefore, are often written with the article prefix **Lu-,** which derives from their names in Luganda rather than the **oru-** of their own names. The Bakiga, for example, call their language Orukiga. However, it is more widely written as Lukiga, is authentic name in Luganda.[4]

The language of the people of Japan in Luganda would be **Lujapani** or, to Bakiga, **Orujapani.** The Luganda names also became adopted by English so that instead of **Orunyankole-Orukiga** the two languages became widely known as **Lunyankole-Lukiga.** These names, though based in Luganda, cannot be wished away because they have become established. Personally, I do not resist these names because they are abundant in literature and history and there is more to gain than lose by retaining them.

In recent years, some scholars in Uganda have renamed such languages as Lunyankole-Lukiga by replacing the Lugandan L with R. Thus, Lunyankole-Lukiga is now known as **Runyankore-Rukiga.** This, in my view, is a disservice to scholarship because no such names exist in the areas where **Orunyankore** and **Orukiga** are spoken. As a result, a false perception has been created that the two languages are called **Runyankore** or **Rukiga** in their respective areas. By replacing the L with R, these revisionist scholars achieved only a semi-truth: they forgot that these names, in the areas where they are spoken, the article prefix **o-** is retained and that, without this, the names lose a vital syllable. In their L-forms the names Lunyankole-Lukiga are as legitimate as the name Uganda itself, which was derived from the Swahili name of the Kingdom of Buganda and adopted into English, complete with the "you" sound in its pronunciation instead of the more Swahili-appropriate one of "woo". Use of Buganda as a name for the region we now know as Uganda was tossed to the wind.

Many other names in Uganda, which have their origins in Lugandan names and English misnomers, remain in use today. Even our commonly used names, Bakiga and Banyankole, are wrong in the context of our language because they are derived from Luganda

---

[4]   *Ru-* and *Oru-* may serve the same purpose as *Lu-* and *Oru-*. Like the Japanese, our Lunyankole-Lukiga is unable to distinguish between L and R except after painful re-training.

and became adopted directly by the English language. *Abakiga* and *Abanyankole* are the correct forms but nobody has ever thought that these should be substituted for the incorrect ones. The Swedish are Svensk and Sweden is Sverige but we in Africa have a habit of blaming even innocent letters and words on colonial plots rather than accepting them for what they are: errors. Clearly, many have seen the presence of these Ls and the inevitable masking of the Rs that followed as proof of Buganda's British agency and domination of the rest of Uganda.

Scholarship respects the historical origins of names and indeed the spirit with which the original European and Bugandan scholars analysed and wrote about our languages. There is no genius at all in revising a name and then producing a result that, in the first place, is just another mutant. For this reason, I have wrought the title of my book from the names Lunyankole-Lukiga. To do otherwise would have been to accept that Rukiga and Runyankore are genuine names in their respective languages. They are not.

The dance of the Bakiga is referred to as Kikiga, with the **ki**-prefix combining with the **-kiga** root to form an adjective in much the same way the *-ish* makes *England* or *Scotland* an adjective. In Lukiga, we can put adjectives to the same use. For example, for *Japanese* we have **ekijapani** and for Belgian we have **ekibirigi,** which derives from the adoptive use of *Belge*. Many Bantu languages have a similar system. Languages in the western region of Uganda have the unique feature of an **o-**prefix for the singular noun in the same way English employs *a* (or *an*) as the article. So, a man is **omu-sheija** and a woman is **omu-kazi**. However, we obtain the respective plural forms of these nouns by substituting **aba-**for **omu-**to obtain **aba-sheija** and **aba-kazi.**

For most of us who speak languages that belong to the Bantu linguistic group in the south of Uganda the terms **aboruganda, oruganda, ruganda** and **enganda,** which are used in reference to languages, people, clans and families, have the same root: **-ganda.** In Luganda, **omuganda** is the word for *a brother* or a person who is born of the same womb as another. For the Baganda, this term was so profound that it became the summative philosophy of their existence when they started their Kingdom of Buganda, or the land of brothers!

Not so in Lunyankole nor in Lukiga, where **omuganda** is the reference to-wait for it-a bundle of sticks. Imagine! However, this is by no means a negative connotation. A popular proverb among Banyankole and Bakiga states, **"Kamwe kamwe nigw'omuganda"**, or, "It is one stick at a time that will make the bundle!" In Lukiga, **oruganda** means a clan and a person of the same clan may be referred to as **o-wo-ruganda.** So, if we marry the two meanings together brothers should huddle like a bundle of sticks! Whatever meaning one prefers to take the name **Uganda** is inspired by a brotherhood bundled together.

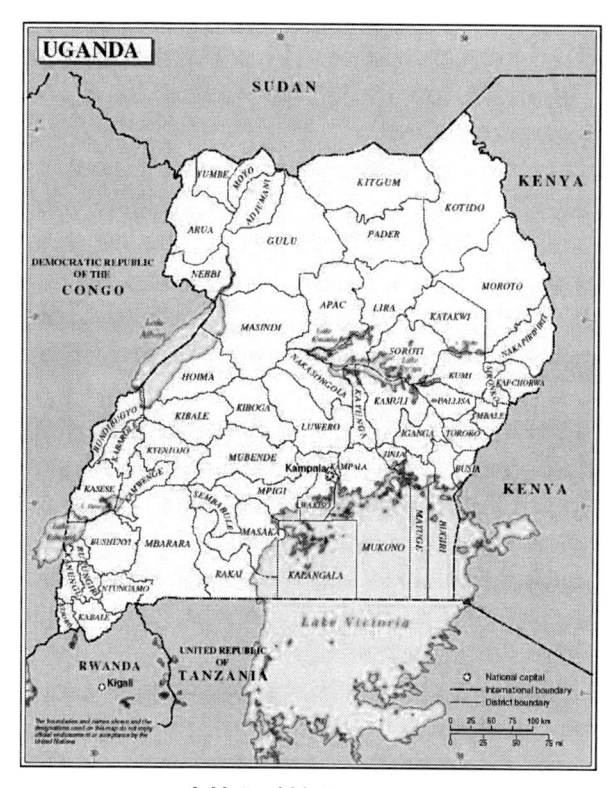

A United Nations map

Uganda ¬ Kigezi is the region directly south of Lake Edward, in a mountainous enclave that encloses Rukungiri, Kanungu, Kabale and Kisoro. It is here that Lukiga is used. The historical Kingdom of Ankole, which includes Mbarara, Ntungamo and Bushenyi, uses a very similar language known as Lunyankole.

Bakiga is the name of the largest linguistic population in Kigezi. Others in the same region are Banyarwanda, who speak Rwandese, or Rwandan, and Bahororo in Northern Kigezi. Basigyi are one of the many clans among the Bakiga. My father, for example, was born into this clan of patrilineal dictates of customs, which make every child born to a Musigyi father a Musigyi. We, Basigyi, are generally abrupt, direct and demanding.

My mother, on the other hand, was born into a calmer, savvier and more pleasant-mannered clan of Barihira. The constituent clans of Kigezi are united in Lukiga, the language that is common to us all and indeed by the cultural mainstream that gives us the same name, Bakiga. All our various subcultures, then, are described by nouns and adjectives derived from the names of our clans. **Kisigyi** or **kirihira,** due to their **ki-**prefix, are adjectives describing the customs and traditions of the named clans.

When the first Church Missionary Society missionaries arrived in Uganda in 1888, they had, amongst them a Bible, a bicycle and a football. Football descended on Uganda for the first time in the form of matches between two teams of Bugandan boys led by, on one side, Dr Albert Ruskin Cook and, on the other, Reverend George Lawrence Pilkington, an impeccable master and enforcer of the rules of the game.

Reverend Pilkington, while serving as a translator and chaplain for the British-led Bugandan army that overthrew Omukama Kabalega from his seat in the Kingdom of Bunyoro, rode his bicycle among the columns of thousands and thousands of men, transmitting messages from the Bugandan soldiers in Luganda to their British commanders in English. Since this introduction, the bicycle has dominated our lives and landscape as a transport vehicle.

George Pilkington, a polymath who also taught fellow missionaries aboard the ship to Mombasa Luganda and tested them repeatedly to ensure that they learned their lessons by the time they arrived in Uganda, had compiled the elements of Luganda grammar. Thus, the Luganda language has had books of grammar for many years. For Lunyankole-Lukiga, this is the first one.

I apologise for errors the reader will find in this book. I would, of course, be grateful for being made aware of them so that the next edition-and there will be one-can be corrected beforehand. Further, I am sorry that not all the Chapters could be accompanied by Lunyankole-Lukiga translations of the technical English headings. This is indeed why such books as these must be written.

Author's Note

I am indebted to Reverend Richard Bewes, former Rector of All Souls Church, Langham Place who, on many occasions after Sunday services, greeted me in Lukiga, unaware that each time he did so and exchanged a few words with me in Lukiga he reminded me that I had a book to complete.

The fact that he, as an Englishman who was born in Kenya, has a keen love of East Africa and was a lifelong friend of my godmother, Miss Lilian Clarke, an English woman who taught my mother and fought for her right to a life-changing bursary, had a bearing on the inspiration I drew from that brief but regular contact with the Reverend Bewes. Stories he told me of his evangelical visits to Uganda often took me back to my childhood and to the memory of two other Englishmen who, like him, had graduated from Cambridge University, albeit at a much earlier time.

I refer here to Dr Algernon "Rugangura" Stanley Smith and his medical college friend, Dr Leonard E "Rutasheka" Sharp, both of whom arrived in Kigezi in 1921. On a hill in Kigezi, the men met my grandfather, Andereya Nduluma, and a memorable friendship began. They taught him how to read and write and, in time, he found their faith attractive and joined their missionary work. I am mindful of the fact that much later, in the late 1960s, Dr Stanley Smith, who had been born in Shanxi, China, where his father arrived as a missionary in 1885 and where I now teach, translated the Bible from English to my language.

My efforts in writing this book are a pale shadow of the work Dr Stanley Smith carried out in achieving such a feat. Even more importantly for me personally both men had fostered and funded my parents' education. My parents loved them as one does a father. It is natural, then, that I should thank them for their efforts and for the benefits that have percolated down to me because of my parents' education and the legacy that education portended for me. There is no educated man or woman in our hills who is not an intellectual descendant of these two men.

In transit visits to my godmother's house in Harrow, London, as I often travelled from the US to Uganda, Miss Clarke encouraged my writing efforts during the earliest stages of this book. Her knowledge of Lukiga, which had astonished me in childhood, helped me to understand how difficult it must have been when she arrived in Kabale in 1942 to learn Lunyankole-Lukiga without a book. Miss Clarke had also aided my father in his work as a historian. Along with her friends, Professor and Mrs David Thomson, formerly of Makerere, she told me how my father carried out distinguished history work on Kigezi. There is no doubt that my father's previous work inspired this project and others that I am yet to complete.

At school in Nairobi, Kenya, a heavily curly-haired Scotsman, G Stavely-Smith, or GSS, as he often signed his names on school merit and demerit cards, taught me to look deeper into the meaning of words in English literature. It was from his class that I first learned etymology, or the study of the origin of words. Unbeknownst to him, this lesson also unleashed an interest that would stretch far beyond English and reach the realm of my thoughts about other languages.

One day, like one who had seen biblical writing on the wall, I was bewildered when a question suddenly posed itself to me. "Why", I asked myself, "was the Latin word *intima,* which means the heart of something and is the origin of such words as *intimate,* close to the Lukiga root **-tima,** which gives us the word **omutima** and also means the heart of something?" Since then, my head has been a hive of questions. That one word alone gave me a scholastic interest in Lukiga that I had not had previously. Writing this book had no scholarly motivation but rather its roots of a distant childhood fascination with human sounds. I am certain that my lifelong dual engagement with English and Lukiga made my interest in either language more acute than it would have been if I had had just one language to learn in childhood.

A story my mother told us after returning from a government mission in the Far-East made a deep impression on me one sunny afternoon in the grounds of a school where she taught: some words in the Japanese language were the same as or similar to others in our language! Later, as we lived among the Giriama, Luo, Kikuyu and Swahili, Lukiga became an increasingly distant voice in the forest of Kenyan languages.

I began to think more objectively about it and to make a quiet, lackadaisical comparative study with other languages in Kenya and Tanzania. I kept neither notes nor tapes but an impressionable mind and exceptional parental resources, who, daily, provided the material that provoked thought and analysis. I was shocked, once during my teenage in Dar-es-salaam, to hear a Tanzanian man from Bukoba, a Muhaya, speaking precisely the same language as us with my father! This was the moment I began to accept that any language was born of mysterious routes of migration. Our languages in East Africa demonstrate a sporadic geography that probably results from historical deposits of themselves along these routes.

While writing English compositions for GSS at school, I realised that even after 6 years of working in an English academic environment, I still did much of my thinking in Lukiga, by now a foreign language in terms of actual daily use. As I did so, I examined and questioned the origin of many words. During the holidays, both my father and mother would continue to confound us with new Lukiga vocabulary, proverbs and expressions that we had not heard before, as if we had never left Kigezi. It was a daily marvel at out dinner table!

One of the topics that recurred in discussions I had with my mother and sister Peace was books we thought we ought to write. My mother, then a committed Civil Servant working out of a government Land-Rover in remote villages of Kigezi, even bought a typewriter and took lessons to start writing in future. Through her work she had a microscopic view of a rural life that was becoming less and less common in our growing urban awareness. There is not a word or pause in this book that has not been inspired by memories of those family thoughts and discussions. To my sister Jean, my only remaining sibling, I have owed affirmation of those historical inspirations.

Yet, there have been many other voices of Banyankole-Bakiga men and women whose explosive sense of humour and cultural pride have, all my life, imbued in me an appreciation of the wonders of Lunyankole-Lukiga. They were Rebecca, my grandmother, and her cousin, Kemitare of Kagarama; Ezrah Mulera; Christopher Bagyeruka; C B Katiti; Benon Bitarabeho; Festo Karwemera; Henry Sebalu; Festo Kivengere; John Bageire; Z Kabaza; Betty Kanyamunyu; Yona

Kanyomoozi; Reverend and Mrs Bitarabeho; Phoebe Rugumayo; Omukyaara Losira; Omwaami Bataringaya; Omwaami Tinzaara; Omwaami Mafigyiri; Omwaami Zaribugyire; Omwaami Bigombe; Omwaami Karwemera; Omwaami Kikira; Omwaami Bamwangyiraki; Omwaami Karekaho-Karegyesa; Omwaami Kakira; Omwaami Zatwoshaho; Omwaami Komukoryo; Omwaami Kyerere; Omwaami Kakuramatsi; Omwaami n'Omukyaara Kikabaheenda; and many, many others.

Without memories of their language, spirit and zest for life in my head, Lukiga would have become a foreign language to me and this book would not have come to fruition.

Edward Nobel Bisamunyu
London, England
July 2011

Chapter One

OUR VOWELS AND CONSONANTS
ENGAMBISA N'ENGAMBISIBWA

The Vowels

As in all the Bantu languages of Africa, vowels are, literally, the most influential letters in Lunyankole-Lukiga. They modify a consonant to produce five different oral sounds or forms of that consonant. For those in the West our vowels would resemble some of those found in the German language.

- **A** as the vowel a in the English word card, bar, or tard
- **E** as the vowel e in the English word end, ember, or enter
- **I** as the sound ee in the English word meet but even shorter, such as India, or indigo
- **O** as the vowel o in the old English word lo, oven, odd or optional
- **U** as the vowel in the German word über or the sound oo in the English word good or the shorter sound in the English words push and put.

For the long forms of these sounds we write the vowel twice. For example, the following nouns: **eibaati** (singular)-an iron sheet; **amabaati** (plural)-iron sheets.

The Consonants

- **B-C-D-F-G-H-J-K-L-M-N-P-R-S-T-V-W-Y-Z-**

The Vowel-Consonant Product

Thus, by using **a,** we can influence **B** to become **Ba.** Or, as in English, to write the impossible sound made by sheep! In the following practice exercise **CA** is pronounced as **CHA**-as in CHAT. We practise these as follows:

- **Ba-Ca-Da-Fa-Ga-Ha-Ja-Ka-La-Ma-Na-Pa-Ra-Sa-Ta-Va-Wa-Ya-Za**

Note that q and x are not represented in our adopted Roman alphabet.

- **A-Ba-Ca-Da-E-Fa-Ga-Ha-I-Ja-Ka-La-Ma-Na-O-Pa-Ra-Sa-Ta-U-Va-Wa-Ya-Za-**

If you practise the following sounds you will have covered the entire range of syllables that enable Lukiga, Lunyankole and many other Bantu languages to construct words. Lukiga, Lunyankole and other Bantu languages in Uganda, Kenya and Tanzania also employ the same system.

- **Ba-Ca-Da-Fa-Ga-Ha-Ja-Ka-La-Ma-Na-Pa-Ra-Sa-Ta-Va-Wa-Ya-Za-**

- **Be-Ce-De-Fe-Ge-He-Je-Ke-Le-Me-Ne-Pe-Re-Se-Te-Ve-We-Ye-Ze-**

The following set is probably the most difficult one for English-speakers to learn. **Bi,** for example, will be pronounced as BE from "To be or not to be". CHI will be like the CHI in the English word CHIN but we often write it as KYI. For English speakers the tendency to pronounce the letter I as EYE always presents problems in producing African sounds when reading written material. Knowing this ahead of the exercise will help one to avoid the error.

- **Bi-Ci-Di-Fi-Gi-Hi-Ji-Ki-Li-Mi-Ni-Pi-Ri-Si-Ti-Vi-Wi-Yi-Zi-**

- **Bo-Co-Do-Fo-Go-Ho-Jo-Ko-Lo-Mo-No-Po-Ro-So-To-Vo-Wo-Yo-Zo-**

- **Bu-Cu-Du-Fu-Gu-Hu-Ju-Ku-Lu-Mu-Nu-Pu-Ru-Su-Tu-Vu-Wu-Yu-Zu-**

PHOTO BY EDWARD NOBEL BISAMUNYU

KIGEZI-ANKOLE BORDER REGION
AHA NIHEIHI N'ENSHARO YA KIGEZI NA ANKOLE

Chapter Two

OUR GREETINGS AND FAREWELLS
ENDAMUKANYA N'ENSIBUURANA

Greetings are an important and elaborate part of our customs in Kigezi. Before we greet somebody we must know where they stand in the hierarchy of relations. This is not to infer that anybody is ever treated as unworthy of respect but everybody is accorded their rightful place of in the greeting process. This is largely determined by a code of respect that is determined by one's age and, therefore, the experience inferred by that age. For example, one stands upon ceremony to greet an older relation. One may have to defer to or invite them to lead in the greeting.

EAST AFRICAN HARBOURS CORPRATION

A MUKIGA WOMAN GREETING FRIENDS AT A PARTY
OMUKIGAKAZI NARAMUSYA BANYWAANIBE AHA KABAGA

A younger relation often cedes "greeting power" to an older relation. I cannot initiate greeting my father when I see him, for example. For having fathered me, my father is granted many privileges, one of which is the right to greet his children but not them to greet him. Similarly, if he has a brother or a half-brother who is younger than his children they come first in the greeting pecking order. Age is not always the determining factor in these matters.

If one is uncertain about one's position in that pecking order one must ask knowledgeable elders present to intervene and decide which of the greeting parties is more senior. Greeting one's in-laws is certainly a very risky issue and one must know one's position or have it determined by knowledgeable elders or one will risk lifelong ridicule!

Greeting

Agandi?	How are you? (Literally: And how is your other news?)
Alternative form of **Agandi** ¬ **Nigaahe?**	This form possibly originates from the use of the word for *where*, **nkahe,** as a way of asking "Where is the good news?"
Nimarungyi.	I am fine. (Literally: It is good news!)
Nigye.	A short and casual form of saying "well". **Gye** in Lukiga means "well." This introduces its use in some of the greetings below. Ni-as a prefix stands for "It is . . ." Thus, **Nigye** means "it is well".
Agandi Sebo?	And your news, Sir?
Agandi Nyabo?	And your news, Madam?
Nimarungyi Sebo.	I am fine, Sir.
Nimarungyi Nyabo.	I am fine, Madam.
Oreire gye?	Good morning! [Literally: Did you sleep well?]
Answer: **Eeego! Shana iwe?**	Yes, and what about you? (Singular)
Or: **Eeego! Shana imwe?**	Yes, what about you? (Plural)

O*s***ibire gye?**	Good day! [Literally: Did you have a good day?]
Answer: **Eeego! *S*hana iwe?**	(Often contracts into **Shaniiwe?**) Yes, and what about you?
Or **Eeego! *S*hana imwe?**	Yes, what about you (plural)?
Kare, ogyeende gye!	Good bye, you (singular) travel safely.
Kare, mugyeende gye!	Good bye to you! Travel safely. (Plural form of "you" is indicated here.)

Greeting forms make little or no literal sense at all in many languages. In English, for example, "Hello!" and "Hi!" infer some sort of recognition but what do they mean?

Forms of greeting in Lunyankole and Lukiga must have had their origins in what familial or familiar people said to one another after long periods of absence. I have never heard the meaning or reasoning of the various greeting forms explained but I have had, on many occasions, reason to think about them myself. Thoughts about their possible origins are given further down, below the greeting forms.

Forms of greeting

To greet/**Okuramusya**
- **Keije?!**

- **Keije?!**
- **Buhooro?!**
- **Buhooro?!**
- **Buhooro gye?!**
- **Agandi?!**

To respond/**Okugarukamu**
- **Eeeh!**
(An abbreviation of Eego!)
- **Eeeh!**
- **Eeeh!**
- **Eeeh!**
- **Eeeh!**
- **Nimarungyi!**

Keije!

This stands for "Welcome!" I suspect it comes from the verb "to come", or **okwiija** or **okweija. Keije** is the imperative form of this verb and therefore means "May you come!" or "Come!" I am convinced that this is equivalent to "Welcome!" which is itself given in imperative form as a means of congratulating one for overcoming the hardships of a journey one is expected or assumed or known to have taken. Given the grave dangers one faced during such journeys in former times, including wild animals that often killed people by stealth, or getting waylaid by one's enemies, such a greeting could not be more appropriate!

Buhooro!

This is another word for "Fine!" **Buhooro,** as in English, means "well" but its original use may have been in reference to a "situation" or "news," which it also describes. The word **amahooro** means news but, given that the stem **-hooro** means "well" **amahooro** may have, initially, referred only to "good news". The Rwandans next door, from whose midst many of the Bakiga are said to have originated, have **amahoro,** which is their word for *news.*

Agandi?

This word really means "Other?" and the reference is to "other news." In its fuller and formal form it is **"Amakuru agandi?"** The word **"amakuru"** is derived from the meaning of important. As an adjective it also refers to **amahurire** or news or "things heard". **Amahurire (amakuru) agandi?** ¬ What other important news (have you)? The "have you" is only inferred but not mentioned.

The approximate translation of the greeting above is this ¬

- "The journey?! The journey?!"

Or,

- "The journey here?!" ¬ Literally, "The coming?"
- The journey here?!"
- Was it well?
- Was it well?

- Was it very well?
- And what about other important news? "**Agandi?**" does not really mean "other news" as in its regular translation but just "others".

Gratitude

There are, in Lunyankole-Lukiga, many expressions of gratitude ranging from the comical to the solemn. These, of course, depend on the familiarity involved between people even though one must remember that Bakiga, in particular, have no respect for decorum! The following phrases apply:

• Thank you!	• **Webare!**
• I have thanked you!	• **Nakusiima!**
• I have thanked you very much!	• **Nakusiima munonga!**
• I thank you!	• **Ninkusiima!**
• I thank you all!	• **Nimbasiima mweena!**
• Thank you very much!	• **Webare munonga!**
• May you have many births! ¬ Giving birth to a child is considered to be the greatest of life's rewards. For this reason the expression of gratitude by such a wish is the ultimate "thank you".	• **Kazaare!**
• May all of you have many births!	• **Nimukazaare!**
• May the Lord bless you!	• **Mukama akuhe omugisha!**
• May the Lord bless you all!	• **Mukama abahe omugisha!**

Farewell

Farewells are less complicated and easier to decipher. People say goodbye to one another in forms based on the verbs to go, to stay or to exist. Some of these forms, as we shall see, do not translate literally. Naturally, as in English, these forms take the imperative sense of a verb.

Some of the farewell forms have been influenced by decades of Christian teaching, which had been a vital source of influence on our language. For simplicity, I have restricted the farewell forms to the Second Person Singular, "You", until other Personal Pronouns are introduced later. The verb *to stay* sometimes resembles the verb *to be strong,* or **okuguma,** *from which it is derived.* They are as follows:

Kare! ¬ **Kare** may have originated from **Kare mbwenu,** which means "Okay then!"

Okay! (Means "Bye!")

Kare, kare!

Okay, okay! (Means "Bye, bye!")

Ogumeho gye! ¬ **O-**stands for the personal pronoun "You!" (Second Person Singular)

You (Second Person Singular) stay on well! Or: You stay on strong!

Ogumeho! ¬ A contraction of the above.

You stay on! Or: You stay strong!

Ogume gye!

You stay well!

Ogyende gye!

You go well!

Obeho gye!

Stay on well! ¬ Literally, "Exist in place well!"

Obe gye!

Stay well! ¬ Literally, "Exist well!"

Mukama akurinde!

May the Lord keep you!

Mukama akwebembere!   May the Lord lead you!

Note that we have the same word for "to stay" and "to be strong". In a culture such as ours, staying in place when there was a war or a climatic upheaval demanded courage. Staying meant putting up resistance and guarding one's own people and property.

Names and Pronouns of Address

In both Lukiga and Lunyankole one can address people using general pronouns like "You" **(Iwe)** for singular or "You" **(Imwe)** for plural. Thus, when you meet a person on the street, you can address them as follows:

- **Agandi iwe?**

Or,

- **Agandi imwe?**

Forgetting people's names is easily forgiven in both languages. One can make up for loss of memory in Lukiga and Lunyankole by using terms of endearment!

One may call a friend "our sibling" or "my dear' or "my son" or "son of Yohaana". A relative may forget one's name but he or she will not forget the affection there is between families. One may use any number of endearment terms in place of names.

- **Mwaana weitu**
- One of our own (children), (infants) or (babies) ¬ [**omwaana** ¬ child, infant, baby] **mutaamba eirungu** ¬ Curer or Healer of Loneliness!
- **Nyakeirungyi**
- Little Owner of Beauty or Little Child of Beauty!

- **Mweene Yohaana**
- Son of Yohaana ¬ Strange as it may seem this is a term of endearment

Thus, one can greet or bid farewell to people using these forms of addresses:

- **Agandi mwaana weitu?**
- **Oṣibire gye mutaamba eirungu?**
- **Kare Nyakeirungyi!**
- **Oreire gye mweene Yohaana?**

Variations

- **Nigaahe? (Nigaaha?)**
- **Ni-**stands for *is* and **-gaahe** or **-gaaha** stands for *which*. This means that **Nigaahe** or **Nigaaha** stands for, literally, "Is which?"

- **Ogumire?**
- ¬ **O-**is a prefix that stands for "you" and **-guma** is a root word that means, literally, tough or hard or strong, referring to a person's health. The suffix **-ire** makes this root word an adjective in much the same way-*ed* makes *hardened* an adjective. This, naturally, seemed to have led to another way of saying "Goodbye". Thus, we say, **"Ogumeho!"**, which is an imperative verb derived from the above, meaning "May you be strong!" or "May you withstand trials!"

- **Nogambaki?**
- Literally, "What do you say?" This derives from an inference to "news" just as **Agandi.** Things you might say will often rate as news depending how long it has been since you last saw somebody so it's natural that they should ask, "What do you have to account for the period of time that has lapsed since our last meeting?"

- **Oragambaki?**
- A common dialect in Kigezi-the land where Lukiga is spoken and which covers several modern districts-is known as Lusigyi. **Oragambaki** is a variation of **Nogambaki.** More about the variance of Lusigyi will be explained later in this book.

A PAINTING BY REBECCA BEBB

REBECCA BEBB (BRIGHTON-HOVE, EAST SUSSEX), GREW UP IN DAR-ES-SALAAM, TANZANIA
EKI KISHUSHAANI (OR EKISHWAANI) KIKAKORWA REBECCA BEBB, OMUNGEREZAKAZI OWA BRIGHTON-HOVE, SUSSEX KWONKA OWAKURIIRE OMURI DAR-ES-SALAAM, TANZANIA

Chapter Three

OUR NUMBERS AND ORDINALS
OKUBARA NOKUBARWA

Numerals and ordinals are very basic of language. We need them to count, tell the time or find our bearings during the week. So, let's learn them first!

NUMERALS

- Zero
- One
- Two
- Three
- Four
- Five
- Six
- Seven
- Eight
- Nine
- Ten
- Eleven
- Twelve
- Thirteen
- Fourteen
- Fifteen

- **Busha**
- **Emwe**
- **Ibiri**
- **Ishatu**
- **Ina**
- **Itano**
- **Mukaaga**
- **Mushanju**
- **Munaana**
- **Mweenda**
- **Ikumi**
- **ikumi neemwe**
- **ikumu na ibiri**
- **ikumi neishatu**
- **ikumi neina**
- **ikumi neitaano**

- Sixteen
- Seventeen
- Eighteen
- Nineteen
- Twenty
- Twenty one

- Twenty two
- Twenty three
- Twenty four
- Twenty five
- Thirty
- Forty
- Fifty
- Sixty
- Seventy
- Eighty
- Ninety
- One hundred
- One hundred and one

- One hundred and two
- One hundred and three
- One hundred and four
- One hundred and five
- One hundred and ten
- One hundred and twenty
- One hundred and thirty
- One hundred and forty

- One hundred and fifty

- One hundred and sixty

- Two hundred

- **ikumu namukaaga**
- **ikumi namushanju**
- **ikumi namunaana**
- **ikumi na mwenda**
- **makumi abiri, or simply, abiri**
- **makumi abiri neemwe; abiri neemwe**

- **makumi abiri neibiri**
- **makumi abiri neishatu**
- **makumi abiri neina**
- **makumi abiri neitaano**
- **makumi ashatu; ashatu**
- **makumi ana; ana**
- **makumi ataano; ataano**
- **makumi mukaaga; nkaaga**
- **makumi mushanju; nshanju**
- **makumi munaana; kinaana**
- **makumi mwenda; kyeenda**
- **Igana**
- **Igana na emwe,** or **Igana neemwe**

- **Igana neibiri**
- **Igana neishatu**
- **Igana neina**
- **Igana neitaano**
- **Igana neikumi**
- **Igana na makumi abiri**

- **Igana na makumi ashatu**
- **Igana na makumi ana [Igana ana]**

- **Igana na makumi ataano [Igana ataano]**

- **Igana na mukumi mukaaga [Igana nkaaga]**

- **Magana abiri**

- Three hundred
- Four hundred
- Five hundred
- Six hundred
- Seven hundred
- Eight hundred
- Nine hundred
- One thousand
- Two thousand
- Three thousand
- Four thousand
- Five thousand
- Ten thousand
- Twenty thousand
- Fifty thousand
- One hundred thousand
- Five hundred thousand
- One million

- **Magana ashatu**
- **Magana ana**
- **Magana ataano**
- **Magana mukaaga**
- **Magana mushaanju**
- **Magana munaana**
- **Magana mweenda**
- **Enkumi emwe**
- **Enkumi ibiri**
- **Enkumi ishatu**
- **Enkumi ina**
- **Enkumi itaano**
- **Omutwaaro gumwe**
- **Emitwaaro ebiri**
- **Emitwaaro etaano**
- **Emitwaaro igana**
- **Emitwaaro magana ataano**
- **Millioni emwe (million'emwe)**

ORDINALS

In Lukiga, ordinal numbers are not straight-forward. Firstly, they are always suffixes attached to the ends of prefixes, which, like pronominal markers, describe the nouns they represent!

- First
- Second
- Third
- Fourth
- Fifth
- Sixth
- Seventh
- Eighth
- Ninth
- Tenth

- **-kubaanza**
- **-kabiri**
- **-kashatu**
- **-kana**
- **-kataano**
- **-mukaaga**
- **-mushaanju**
- **-munaana**
- **-mweenda**
- **-kumi**

After the "first" one, the ordinal roots correspond to their numerals. In other words, the first ordinal root, **-kubaanza,** is the only one that seems to deviate from having something in common with the corresponding numeral.

The possessive prefix that joins the subject and its adjective is determined by the noun group the subject represents. If, for example, we are talking about "the first person", we say, **Omuntu wa-okubaanza** but this contracts into **Omuntu w'-okubaanza.** If we are talking about "the first people" we say **abantu bo-kubaanza,** contracting this into **abantu b'-okubaanza.**

We can see that the prefixes that stand for possessive pronouns match the nouns they are describing quite specifically:

- **Omuntu wa oku-baanza,** which contracts into **omuntu w'okubaanza**
- **Omuntu wa ka-biri**
- **Omuntu wa ka-shatu**
- **Ekitabo ky'okubaanza**
- **Ekitabo kya ka-biri**
- **Ekitabo kya ka-shatu**
- **Ebitabo by'okubaanza**
- **Ebitabo bya kabiri**
- **Ebitabo bya kashatu**
- **Embwa y'oukubaanza**
- **Embwa z'okubaanza**

Practice Exercise

Numbers, as in English, may also serve as adjectives. They describe nouns so that we know how many of them there are. In Lunyankole-Lukiga, an adjective must conform to the noun it is describing by taking the grouping-prefix of that noun.

If we are discussing a book, **ekitabo,** for example, or books, **ebitabo,** we must apply the appropriate group-prefix for all the nouns in the same noun group. The correct group-prefix depends on whether we are talking about the singular form or the plural form of a noun.

Ekitabo, or **ebitabo,** belong to the **Eki-Ebi** Noun Group. As we can see, the **Eki-** is the prefix for the singular form of the noun and the **Ebi-** is the prefix for the plural. Their group "descriptive prefixes", however, are **ki-** and **bi-** respectively. This means that in order to write anything about them to describe their number or colour or size we must apply **ki-** or **bi-.** Thus, for a book (one book) we say **ekitabo ki-mwe.** For two books we say **ebitabo bi-biri.**

This topic will be covered more fully elsewhere in this book but it will help to have an advance view while one is learning numbers for the first time.

Noun	Noun group (singular and plural respectively)	Group descriptive prefixes (singular and plural respectively) ¬ Example	English Translation
Omuntu/ Abantu Person/people	**Omu-/aba-**	**o-/ba-**¬ **Omuntu omwe, abantu babiri**	One person, two people
Ekitabo/ Ebitabo Book/books	**Eki-/ebi-**	**ki-/bi-**¬ **ekitabo kimwe, ebitabo bibiri**	One book, two books
Embwa/ Embwa Dog/dogs	**E-/e-**	**E-/i-**¬ **embwa emwe, embwa ibiri**	One dog, two dogs

Akati/Obuti A small stick/ small sticks	**Aka-/obu-**	**Aka-/obu-¬ akati kamwe, obuti bubiri**	One small stick, two small sticks
Eicumu/ amacumu One spear, two spears	**Ei-/Ama-**	**Ei-/ama-¬ eicumu rimwe, amacumu abiri**	One spear, two spears

Chapter Four

THE LUNAR CALENDAR
OKWEEZI KUMWE

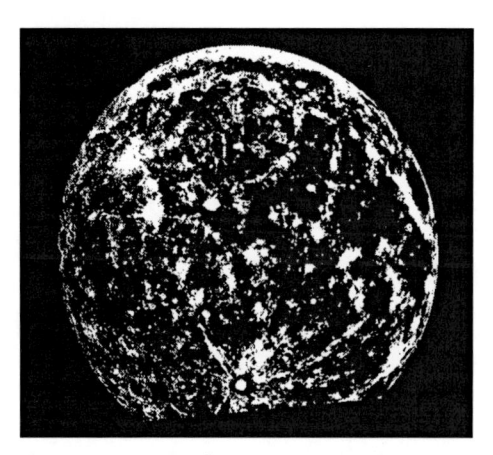

NASA ¬ http://antwrp.gsfc.nasa.gov/apod/ap020316.html

THE MOON
OKWEEZI

RELEVANT VOCABULARY

- **Erizooba**
- **Erizooba ni**

- Today
- Today is

- **Nyomwebazyo** • Yesterday

- **Nyenkyakare** or **nyensakare** • Tomorrow
- **Omukasheeshe** • In the morning

- **Omwihaangwe** • In the mid-afternoon

- **Omumwebaazyo** • In the late afternoon

- **Esabiiti erikwiija** • Next week ¬ Literally, the week that is coming

- **Esabiiti eyahweire** • Last week ¬ Literally, the week that has ended

- **Omweezi ogurikwiija** • Next month ¬ Literally, the month that is coming

- **Okweezi oku** • This month

- **Omweezi ogwahweire** • Last month ¬ Literally, the month that has ended

- **Omwaaka ogu** • This year

- **Omwaaka ogurikwiija** • Next year

- **Omwaaka ogwahweire** • Last year

- **Burizooba, buriijo** • Always

- **Obumwe, rimwe na rimwe** • Sometimes, occasionally

Days of the Week

Our days of the week are different from the British calendar from which we derive many usages, including the notions of a seven-day week and a thirty-day month. Our week, for some reason, begins with Monday rather than Sunday. I suspect this has its origins in the European work week, which began with Monday. It was through the process of European employment of African labour that many practices have their beginning. Thus, we call Monday by a name that literally proclaims it as "the first day of the week". We are not alone in this because the practice is widespread throughout East Africa and beyond.

- **Orwokubaanza**   • Monday
- **Orwakabiri**   • Tuesday
- **Orwakashatu**   • Wednesday
- **Orwakana**   • Thursday
- **Orwakataano**   • Friday
- **Orwamukaaga**   • Saturday
- **Sabiiti/Saande**   • Sunday

As in English, prepositions help to say when an action is taking place. So, we say,

- **Aharwokubaanza**   • on Monday
- **Aharwakabiri**   • on Tuesday
- **Aharwakashatu**   • on Wednesday
- **Aharwakana**   • on Thursday
- **Aharwakataano**   • on Friday
- **Aharwamukaaga**   • on Saturday
- **Ahasabiiti**   • on Sunday

Practise with these examples. The monotony is a deliberate ploy to keep sentences as simple and repetitive as possible until more is known about sentence construction:

1. **Ninyija/*ndeija* kwiija aharwakabiri.** ¬ I will come on Tuesday.

2. **Ninyija/*ndeija* kugyenda aharwakabiri.** ¬ I will go on Tuesday.
3. **Ninyija/*ndeija* kugaruka aharwakataano.** ¬ I will return on Friday.
4. **Ninyija/*ndeija* kutayaaya aharwakataano.** ¬ I will visit on Friday.
5. **Ninyija/*ndeija* kumara aharwakataano.** ¬ I will complete on Friday.
6. **Omukade**[5] **naija/*areija* kwiija *erizooba*.** ¬ The priest will come *today*. (As in English today, which in Lunyankole-Lukiga means, literally, this day, does not need a preposition!)
7. **Omwaami Tinkasiga naija/*areija* kwiija aharwakashatu.** ¬ Mr Tinkasiga will come on Wednesday.
8. **Mutaahi wangye naija/*areija* kugyeenda aharwakana.** ¬ My neighbour will leave (go) on Thursday.
9. **Omupiira gwa Premier League nigwiija/*gureija* kutandika aharwamukaaga.** ¬ The Premier Football League will start on Saturday.
10. **John neija/*areija* kwiija aharwamukaaga.** ¬ John will come on Saturday.

English days of the week are frequently used as names of children in East Africa. The most common of these are Sunday, Monday, Friday and Saturday!

Months of the Year

• January	• **Jenwari**
• February	• **Febwari**
• March	• **Maachi**
• April	• **Eppo**
• May	• **Meyi**

---

[5] **Omukade** is a Christian church priest. This word is derived from a Luganda word, **omukadde,** which means an elderly person but also infers that that person is endowed with uncommon wisdom and experience. In Luganda, indeed as in many other African languages, age comes with wisdom.

- June
- July
- August
- September
- October
- November
- December

- **Juni**
- **Julayi**
- **Ogasita/Ogasiti**
- **Seputemba**
- **Okitoba**
- **Novemba**
- **Desemba**

More generally, however, the twelve months of the year are referred to by their ordinal positions. The word **okweezi** means both *moon* and *month*. Each word following **okweezi** in the list below is an adjective (see the underlined part) that gives the ordinal number or position of each month after the relevant descriptive prefix.

January	**Jenwari**	**okweezi kwokubaanza**
February	**Febwari**	**okweezi kwakabiri**
March	**Maachi**	**okweezi kwakashatu**
April	**Eppo**	**okweezi kwakana**
May	**Meyi**	**okweezi kwakataano**
June	**Juni**	**okweezi kwamukaaga**
July	**Julayi**	**okweezi kwamushaanju**
August	**Ogasita/Ogasiti**	**Ogasita ¬ okweezi kwamunaana**
September	**Seputemba**	**Seputemba ¬ okweezi kwamwenda**
October	**Okitoba**	**Okitoba ¬ okweezi kweikumi**

November	**Novemba**	**Novemba ¬ okweezi kweikuminakumwe** (The **-ku-** in the box here is a descriptive prefix referring to the nouns in the same group as months. We shall discuss these in a later chapter.)
December	**Desemba**	**Desemba ¬ okweezi kweikumineibiri** (Technically, we should say **okweezi kweikuminakubiri** but we do not!)

Month in English	Month in Lukiga as derived from English	Month in Lukiga as derived from ordinals
January	**Jenwari**	**okweezi kwokubaanza**
February	**Febwari**	**okweezi kwakabiri**
March	**Maachi**	**okweezi kwakashatu**
April	**Epo**	**okweezi kwakana**
May	**Meyi**	**okweezi kwakataano**
June	**Juni**	**okweezi kwamukaaga**
July	**Julayi**	**okweezi kwamushaanju**

August	**Ogasita** or **Ogasti**	**okweezi kwamunaana**
September	**Seputemba**	**okweezi kwamwenda**
October	**Okitoba**	**okweezi kweikumi**
November	**Novemba**	**okweezi kweikuminakumwe**
December	**Desemba**	**okweezi kweikumineibiri**

A Short Exercise

Q: **Erizooba nebiro bingahe?**
A: **Erizooba n'ebiro mushaanju.**

What is the date today?

Q: **Erizooba norwakangahe?**
A: **Erizooba norwamukaaga.**

What is the day of the week today?

Q: **Omu mwaaka harimu emyeezi engahe?**
A: **Omumwaaka harimu emyeezi ikumi neibiri.** ¬ A variation of this will be **ikumi neebiri,** with the third **i** replaced by an **e.**

How many months are there in a year?

Q: **Oku nokweezi kwa kangahe?**
A: **Oku kweenzi nokwamunaana.**

What month is this?

Q: **Hati turi omukweezi kwangahe?**
A: **Hati turi omukweezi kwamweenda.**

What month are we in now?

Q: **Iwe okazaarwa omu kweezi kwa kangahe?**
A: **Nyowe nkazaarwa omukweezi kwamushaanju.**

In what month were you born?

Years

- The year 1968
- **Omwaaka rukumi rwenda na nkaaga munaana**

- The year 2010
- **Omwaaka bikumi bibiri n'eikumi**

Chapter Five

TELLING THE TIME
ESHAAHA ZEITU

PHOTO BY EDWARD NOBEL BISAMUNYU

BIG BEN, HOUSES OF PARLIAMENT, LONDON
BIG BEN, AHAMAJU GORUKIIKO RWEIHANGA, LONDON

The 12-hour clock is relatively new in East Africa. In many places its use will have been in existence for just over 100 years.

On the 12-hour clock time is read quite differently to English in all our languages in East Africa. Instead of starting with the hour after midnight as the first unit of time, we begin with the first hour after dawn, which was assumed long ago to be the first hour after 6 am. Thus, our 7.00 a.m. is, literally, 1.00 a.m. Midday is 6.00 noon and 12 midnight is 6.00 midnight! Our 4.00 pm, or 16.00 hours, is 10.00 pm.

This is a common feature in all of East Africa and, I suspect, throughout the African continent. It is admirable then that, as young children, Africans in East Africa learn to tell the time in two versions: East African time-telling and "British" time-telling. Very likely, the East African time-telling feature has its origins in an attempt at simplification. With us in Africa the day begins at dawn and so it must have made sense then that a clock should begin at the same time as day! Now, of course, we have two complex systems working side by side so well that one does not get lost in translation from one system to another.

The following vocabulary will help you to learn how to tell the time:

- **Eshaaha** • the time, hour or hours, the clock, a watch
- **Shaaha** • the common contraction of **eshaaha**
- **Hati** • Now (Not always used but as in English the "now" is implied in "The time is ...")
- **Ni** • It is ...
- **Na** • And
- **Edakiika** • Minutes

- **Esekenda** • Seconds
- **Ekichweeka** • a half
- **Omukasheeshe** • in the morning
- **Omwihaangwe** • in the mid-afternoon
- **Omumwebazyo** • in the afternoon
- **Ya** • of: "Ya" is a possessive adjective (of a single hour)
- **Za** • of: "Za" is the possessive adjective (of several hours)

The Time Question!

- **Ni shaaha zingahe hati?** Or: **Hati ni shaaha zingahe?**
  • What's the time now? Literally: How many hours is it now? Or: Now, how many hours is it?

- **Hati, ni shaaha emwe.**
  • Now, it is seven o'clock.

- **Hati, ni shaaha emwe y'omukasheeshe.**
  • Now, it is seven o'clock in the morning. Literally: It is now one hour of the morning.

- **Ni shaaha ikumi n'emwe n'ekichweeka z'omukasheeshe.**
  • It is half past five in the morning.

- **Ni shaaha mushaanju n'edakiika ikumi n'eitano.**
  • It is ten past one.

A Short Exercise

- **Ni shaaha emwe.**
- **Ni shaaha ibiri.**
- **Ni shaaha ishatu.**
- **Ni shaaha ina.**
- **Ni shaaha itaano.**
- **Ni shaaha mukaaga.**
- **Ni shaaha mushaanju.**
- **Ni shaaha munaana.**
- **Ni shaaha mwenda.**
- **Ni shaaha ikumi.**
- **Ni shaaha ikumi n'emwe.**
- **Ni shaaha ikumi n'eibiri.**

- It is seven o'clock.
- It is eight o'clock.
- It is nine o'clock.
- It is ten o'clock.
- It is eleven o'clock.
- It is twelve o'clock.
- It is one o'clock.
- It is two o'clock.
- It is three o'clock.
- It is four o'clock.
- It is five o'clock.
- It is six o'clock.

Photo by Edward Nobel Bisamunyu

Time for tennis at Wimbledon, London, 2010
Eshaaha zakapiira ka tenesi omuri Wimbledon, London, 2010

Ni Shaaha Zingahe Hati?

- **Ni shaaha emwe n'edakiika ina.**
- **Ni shaaha ibiri n'edakiika ikumi.**
- **Ni shaaha ishatu n'edakiika ikumi n'eitaano.**
- **Ni shaaha ina n'edakiika ikumi na munaana.**
- **Ni shaaha itaano nekichweeka.**
- **Ni shaaha mukaaga n'edakiika makumi ashatu n'eitaano.**
- **Ni shaaha mushaanju n'edakiika makumi ana.**
- **Ni shaaha munaana n'edakiika makumi ana n'eitaano.**
- **Ni shaaha mwenda n'edakiika ikumi n'eibiri.**
- **Ni shaaha ikumi n'edakiika ikumi na mwenda.**
- **Ni shaaha ikumi n'emwe n'edaakika makumi abiri.**
- **Ni shaaha ikumi n'eibiri nekichweeka.**

- It is seven o'clock and four minutes.
- It is ten past eight.
- It is a quarter past nine.
- It is eighteen minutes past ten.
- It is a half past eleven.
- It is twenty-five minutes to one.
- It is twenty minutes to two.
- It is a quarter to three.
- It is twelve past three.
- It is nineteen minutes past four.
- It is twenty minutes past five.
- It is a half past six.

Time in English	Denoted Time in Lukiga	Spoken Time in Lukiga
12 midnight	6 hours of the night or 6th hour of the night	**Shaaha mukaaga zekiro.**
1 am	7 hours of the night or 7th hour of the night	**Shaaha mushanju zekiro.**
2 am	8 hours of the night or 7th hour of the night	**Shaaha munaana zekiro.**
3 am	9 hours of the night or 7th hour of the night	**Shaaha mweenda zekiro.**
4 am	10 hours of the night or 7th hour of the night	**Shaaha ikumi zekiro.**
5 am	11 hours of the night or 7th hour of the night	**Shaaha ikumi neemwe zekiro.**
6 am	12 hours of the night or 7th hour of the night	**Shaaha ikumi neibiri zekiro.**
7 am	1 hour of the day or 1st hour of the day	**Shaaha emwe y'omukasheeshe.**
8 am	2 hours of the day or 2nd hour of the day	**Shaaha ibiri z'omukasheeshe.**
9 am	3 hours of the day or 3rd hour of the day	**Shaaha ishatu z'omukasheeshe.**
10 am	4 hours of the day or 4th hour of the day	**Shaaha ina z'omukasheeshe.**
11 am	5 hours of the day or 5th hour of the day	**Shaaha itaano z'omukasheeshe.**
12 am (noon)	6 hours of the day or 6th hour of the day	**Shaaha mukaaga z'omwihaangwe.**
1 pm	1 hour of the day or 7th hour of the day	**Shaaha mushanju z'omwihaangwe.**
2 pm	8 hours of the day or 8th hour of the day	**Shaaha munaana z'omwihaangwe.**
3 pm	9 hours of the day or 9th hour of the day	**Shaaha mwenda z'omwihaangwe.**
4 pm	10 hours of the day or 10th hour of the day	**Shaaha ikumi z'omwihaangwe.**

5 pm	11 hours of the day or 11th hour of the day	**Shaaha ikumi nemwe z'omumwebazyo.**
6 pm	12 hours of the day or 12th hour of the day	**Shaaha ikumi neibiri z'omumwebazyo.**
7 pm	1 hour of the night or 1st hour of the night	**Shaaha emwe y'ekiro.**
8 pm	2 hours of the night or 2nd hour of their night	**Shaaha ibiri z'ekiro.**
9 pm	3 hours of the night or 3rd hour of their night	**Shaaha ishatu z'ekiro.**
10 pm	4 hours of the night or 4th hour of their night	**Shaaha ina z'ekiro.**
11 pm	5 hours of the night or 5th hour of their night	**Shaaha itano z'ekiro.**
12 am	6 hours of the night or 6th hour of their night	**Shaaha mukaaga z'ekiro.**

In ancient times we, in Kigezi, Ankole and elsewhere in East Africa, told the time by estimating the sun's position in the sky. No doubt time-telling was a very crude business then. However, it did not obscure our day's objectives of tilling the land, sowing seeds, weeding and harvesting the crops by that universal evening hour: the gloaming!

Photo by Edward Nobel Bisamunyu

The sun rising over the vast valleys of Kabale, Kigezi, SW Uganda
Omushana nigutandika kujwa burikusheesha omuruhanga rwa Kabale

Chapter Six

OUR PERSONAL PRONOUNS
EBIKUBYO BYEITU

As in English, personal pronouns function as markers of identification of the main subject in a sentence in Lunyankole-Lukiga. However, they are always accompanied by additional prefixes, as I shall explain shortly. In effect, the personal pronoun in question does not often exist by itself.

In fact, one may see it as the appendage "am" when the English First Person Singular, "I", is used in the Present Tense. The difference, of course, is that in English "am" is an indication of a current action involving the verb "to be", or, perhaps more simply, as a product of conjugation of the verb *to be*.

In Lunyankole-Lukiga, the post-pronoun prefixes I have mentioned are in place to affirm the pertinent personal pronoun and they always precede the object-verb complex in a sentence, as we shall see later.

Let us deal with the personal pronouns proper first:

- **Nyowe**
- **Iwe**
- **We** (read *way*, as in "the *way* to London") ¬ Very gender neutral!

- I
- You (singular)
- He/She [Yes! We have one pronoun for both male and female!]

- **Itwe**
- **Imwe**
- **Bo** (pronounced with aspiration so that it sounds as **b-h-o)**

- We
- You (plural)
- They

Pronouns, surprisingly, are universal in human languages. They are useful in making sentences not least because they are easy to apply as subjects without using names. However, we also use them as objects in sentences. In English, for example, "*She* gave the book to *me*" includes "She" as a personal subject pronoun and "me" as an object pronoun. These, of course, also have relevant plural forms and collective knowledge of them facilitates readier application of a language, whether that is English or Lunyankole-Lukiga.

Let us examine subject pronouns and object pronouns and how they function in Lunyankole-Lukiga. First, however, a brief look at an English sentence will give one firm ground for understanding equivalent use in Lunyankole-Lukiga.

If I say, "I love you", I have used the subject pronoun "I" and the object pronoun "you". In English, we say that the verb between "I" and "you" describes a relational process or action between them. Subject "I" loves object "you".

Lunyankole-Lukiga has precisely the same sort of usage so that one says **Nyowe ninkukuunda. Nyowe** is the subject pronoun "I" and the first-**ku**-midfix indicates the object pronoun "you". As seen before, the **ni-**at the beginning of the second phrase-it's not a word, even though it looks like one, because it has many elements in it that actually represent the equivalent of several words in English-indicates the Present Tense.

It is at the end of the object pronoun that the operative verb, **-kuunda,** is found.

Singular

PERSONAL PRONOUNS
- **Iwe** ¬ you
- **We** ¬ he
- **We** ¬ she

- **Kyo** ¬ it

RELATED OBJECT FORMS
- **-ku-**
- **-mu-** or **-mwa-** ¬ him
- **-mu-** or **-mwa-** ¬ her
- **-gi-** or **-ki-** or **-kya-** ¬ it: Note that this will depend on the noun group to which the object in question belongs. We shall discuss noun groups in detail in a later chapter.

Plural

PERSONAL PRONOUNS
- **Itwe** ¬ we
- **Imwe** ¬ you
- **Bo** ¬ they ¬ "They", here, stands for human beings only! This means that, unlike in English, animals and inanimate objects come under different pronouns. I will introduce those later in this chapter.

RELATED OBJECT PRONOUNS
- **-tu-** ¬ us
- **-ba-** ¬ you

- **-ba-** ¬ them

AN EXAMPLE:

- **Omushaho aka-tu-kyebera.** ¬ The doctor examined us. (**Okukyebera** ¬ to examine, to inspect)

Instead of "The doctor examined us" we can say "He inspected us". Similarly, in Lunyankole-Lukiga, we say, **We a-ka-tu-kyebera.** I shall explain the **a-**prefix in another Chapter but let it suffice to say, for the moment, that it is an integral part of the personal pronoun **WE.**

As in English the subject pronouns serve to represent the topical items of sentences and the object pronouns serve as the active "targets" of the subjects. For example, "The man outran the dog", or "He outran the dog". We can say, naturally, in Lunyankole-Lukiga, **"Omushaija akasiga embwa"**, or **"We akasiga embwa"**. Here, **"We"** replaces **Omushaija.** Further, we can replace *the dog,* **embwa,** with the midfix **-gi-** as the object pronoun: **"We aka-gi-siga"**.

Each of the pronouns given above takes a corresponding verb-prefix, which means, quite simply, that it is attached before the verb but has nothing to do with its conjugation or meaning.

- **Nyowe n-**
- **Iwe o-**
- **We a-**
- **Itwe tu-**
- **Imwe mu-**
- **Bo ba-**

- I
- You (singular)
- He/She
- We
- You (plural)
- They

From the verb "to be", **okuba,** which, as in English, is highly irregular, we obtain the suffix **-ri.** This, then, should come after the prefixes I have mentioned above. So, we have,

- **Nyowe ni-ri** ¬ I have crossed through this to show that it actually does not exist in this form. However, I believe it to derive from it. **Nyowe ndi-**

- This however, is not true! Probably because pronouncing **ni-ri** would have been laborious during the evolution of the language it became **Nyowe n-di,** a much less awkward proposition of pronunciation than **Nyowe niri,** I think.

- **Iwe o-ri**

- You are

- **We a-ri**

- He/She is

- **Itwe tu-ri**
- **Imwe mu-ri**
- **Bo ba-ri**

- We are
- You (plural) are
- They are

Examples of simple sentences

- **Nyowe ndigye.**
- **Iwe origye.**
- **We arigye.**

- I am well.
- You [singular] are well.
- He/She is well. This pronoun is gender neutral!

- **Itwe turigye.**
- **Imwe murigye.**
- **Bo barigye.**

- We arigye.
- You (plural) are well.
- They are well.

We can be less formal in speech by dropping the personal pronoun proper altogether and let the verb-prefix stand in its place, as I have shown below:

- **Ndigye.**
- **Origye.**
- **Arigye.**

- I am well.
- You [singular] are well.
- He/She is well. This prefix, like the pronoun it stands for, is gender neutral!

- **Turigye.**
- **Murigye.**
- **Barigye.**

- We arigye.
- You (plural) are well.
- They are well.

"They", "them" and "their": Animals and Inanimate Objects

PERSONAL PRONOUNS

They

- Byo
- Zo

OBJECT PRONOUNS

- **-bi-**e.g. **Byo ni-tu-bi-guza.**
- **-zi-**e.g. **Zo ni-tu-zi-guza.**

Chapter Seven

Our Verbs
Enkora

Infinitive verbs in Lunyankole-Lukiga begin with the prefix oku-. For example: **okureeba** ¬ to see, **okubara** ¬ to count, etc.

Many verbs in Lunyankole-Lukiga are derived from pre-exisiting verbs in much the same way English creates new ones by adding prepositions. For example, *to cut*, we can derive the verb *to cut for*. In Lunyankole-Lukiga, we apply suffixes to the end of a verb to modify its meaning. For example, **okushara** means to cut but we can transform this into "cut for" by removing the vowel at the end, **-a** in this case, and attaching **-ira.**

Similarly, we can make "to be cut for" [as in "A key has been cut for me"] by attaching the suffix **-irwa** at the end of **okushara.** I will add some of these modified verbs in the table of verbs below. Other suffixes are possible but are not discussed here for the sake of brevity. However, they can be found attached to the relevant verbs in the table below.

Infinitive verb	Translation
• Okuba/okutaba	• to be/not to be
• Okubaaga	• To butcher
• Okubaanda	• to stampede
• Okubandama	• to lie down (in prostration)

- **Okubanza** • To start, to initiate
- **Okubaziira** • to sew
- **Okubeiha** • to tell lies
- **Okubeija** • To do carpentry work, to sculpt
- **Okubiinga** • To dispel, to dismiss, to expel
- **Okubona** • To find
- **Okubonabona** • To suffer ¬ literally ¬ to find or meet with over and over again
- **Okubumbata/ okufumbata** • To hug
- **Okubura; okuburira; okuburirwa** • To disappear, to hide, to be scared; to be lost to; to be lost in
- **Okubuunga** • To roam
- **Okubuuza; okubuzibwa** • To ask; to be asked or to be given an examination
- **Okuchureera** • To be quiet, like a child; to be mild
- **Okuchurika** • To turn upside-down
- **Okuchwa** • To cut off, to tear, to ostracise
- **Okuchwa** • To cut, to tear, to rip up
- **Okuchwaho** • To cut off, to tear off, to ostracise
- **Okuchwanyagura** • To tear up something into small pieces
- **Okufa** • To die
- **Okufayo** • To care about something
- **Okufundikira** • To place the lid on
- **Okufundiza** • To crowd, to squeeze into a corner
- **Okufungura** • To dilute (a drink, for example)
- **Okuhagaaga** • To harass, to be a nuisance to others
- **Okugaamba** • To talk, to speak, to say
- **Okugaamba** • To speak, to sound

- **Okugaaya** — To sigh
- **Okugaba** — To give freely
- **Okuganiira** — To converse
- **Okuganira** — To tell a story to somebody
- **Okugaruka** — to return, to come back
- **Okugarukayo** — To return somewhere
- **Okugarura** — To bring back, to vomit
- **Okugaya** — To despise
- **Okuguma** — To be firm, to remain firm
- **Okuguruka** — To jump, to fly
- **Okuguza** — To sell
- **Okugwa** — To fall
- **Okugweera** — To lie in wait for something
- **Okugyenda** — To go
- **Okuha** — To give
- **Okuhaanda** — To treat people aggressively
- **Okuhaanga** — To create
- **Okuhabura** — To advise
- **Okuhaburwa** — To be advised
- **Okuhakana** — To debate, to argue
- **Okuhandiika** — To write
- **Okuharara** — To crave the unusual, to drop old things unreasonably for new ones
- **Okuheeka** — To carry a baby
- **Okuhemuka** — To be ashamed
- **Okuheruruka** — To see last (last time to see)
- **Okuhiiga** — To hunt
- **Okuhika** — To reach, to arrive
- **Okuhinduka** — To turn around, to change
- **Okuhinga** — To cultivate, to grow (plants), to dig
- **Okuhisya** — To make to reach or arrive
- **Okuhonoka** — To drop off (e.g. a fruit off a tree)
- **Okuhoora enzigu** — To exact revenge
- **Okuhora** — To cool down (of a drink or food)

- **Okuhoza**
- **Okuhunama**
- **Okuhungurira**

- **Okuhurira**
- **Okuhwa**

- **Okujuguta**
- **Okujuma**
- **Okujumiṣa**
- **Okujuna**
- **Okujwaara**
- **Okujwaara**
- **Okujweeka**
- **Okukaranga**
- **Okukinga**
- **Okukookoota**
- **Okukora**
- **Okukorora**
- **Okukunda**
- **Okukura**
- **Okukurura**
- **Okukuza**
- **Okumanya**
- **Okumanyana**
- **Okumweenya**
- **Okunaaba**
- **Okunaaba**
- **Okunabiiṣa**
- **Okunaga**
- **Okunena**

- **Okuniga**
- **Okunyaama**
- **Okunyaga**
- **Okunyatuura**
- **Okunywa**
- **Okunywaana**

- To judge a legal case
- To be silent
- To succeed, as in when one inherited a late brother's wife
- To hear
- To be completed (milk, bread, tea for example)
- To throw, to toss
- To abuse, to mistreat
- To cause to abuseor mistreat
- To save, to rescue
- To dress, to put on
- To put on
- To dress somebody
- To fry, to roast
- To shut, to close
- To wrinkle with age, to age
- To make, to do
- To cough
- To love, to like
- to grow
- To pull
- to bring up
- to know
- To know one another
- To smile (subtly only!)
- To wash oneself
- To wash, to bathe, to shower
- To wash somebody
- To lose something
- To nibble or crunch between teeth
- To strangle
- To sleep, to lie down
- To rob, to fail to pay a debt
- To eat voraciously
- To drink
- To make friends

- **Okupakaza** • To work or labour for pay
- **Okupapaza** • To flap (wings, for example)
- **Okuraara** • To spend the night
- **Okuraara** • To grow wild (for a bush)
- **Okurahuka** • To hurry
- **Okurahura** • To annoy, to disturb
- **Okurasha** • To shoot
- **Okurasha** • To shoot
- **Okureeba** • To see
- **Okureenga** • To overflow, to overwhelm
- **Okureesa** • To smoke
- **Okureeta** • To bring
- **Okurekyera** • To throw, to toss
- **Okuremeera** • To be heavy
- **Okuriisa** • To feed, to graze (animals)
- **Okuringaana** • To balance
- **Okurira** • To cry
- **Okurusya** • To bother, to disturb, to vex, to annoy
- **Okurotama** • To crouch
- **Okuruka** • To knit, to weave
- **Okuruma** • To bite
- **Okurwaana** • To fight, to struggle
- **Okurwaana** • To fight
- **Okurwanira** • To fight for
- **Okurya** • To eat
- **Okusa** • To mill
- **Okusasira** • To forgive
- **Okushaasha/okusaasa** • To feel pain
- **Okushaba** • To pray, to ask
- **Okushagiza** • To crowd somebody, to cause problems for
- **Okushaka** • To search for food
- **Okushamaara** • To gawk, to stare, to gape
- **Okushanga** • To find, to stumble upon something
- **Okushara** • To cut, to cut off
- **Okusheemba** • To support

- **Okusheemba** — To be last in something
- **Okusheenya** — To destroy, to break, to smite
- **Okusheenyagura** — To destroy
- **Okusheka** — To laugh
- **Okushekura** — To pound something with mortar and pestle
- **Okushemererwa** — To be happy
- **Okushenyagurika** — To fall to pieces, to crumble
- **Okushereka** — To hide
- **Okushitama/Okusitama** — To sit
- **Okushoba** — To be complicated, to be difficult (to solve)
- **Okushoba** — To be complicated, to be a problem
- **Okushoberwa** — To worry, to be concerned
- **Okushoborora** — To explain, to unravel
- **Okushohora** — To go out of the house
- **Okushohora** — To go out, to exit, to go on a short errand
- **Okushohoza** — To take something out of the house
- **Okushoma** — To read
- **Okushoomba** — To harvest, to gather
- **Okushora** — To pay tax
- **Okusiga** — To leave behind
- **Okusigara** — To remain
- **Okusiima** — To thank, or to give thanks
- **Okusiimwa** — To be thanked
- **Okusya** — To ripen or to become ready
- **Okusyaaza** — To sharpen (a knife)
- **Okuta** — To put
- **Okutaaha** — To return home, to enter
- **Okutabaara** — To announce an emergency
- **Okutambura** — To walk, to roam
- **Okutandika** — To begin, to pioneer
- **Okutangaara** — To be filled with wonder
- **Okutangaaza** — To find something wonderful

- **Okutaragaza, okutabaguza**
- **Okutayaaya**
- **Okutebeekana**
- **Okuteeka**
- **Okuteekateka**
- **Okuteemba**
- **Okuteera**
- **Okuteera orwari**
- **Okuteerana**
- **Okutegaana**
- **Okuteguura**
- **Okutegyeerera**
- **Okutegyeereza**
- **Okutema; okutemwa**
- **Okutemburuka**
- **Okutemurura**
- **Okuterana**
- **Okuteranira**
- **Okutereka**
- **Okutetema**
- **Okutiina**
- **Okutiina**
- **Okutoora**
- **Okutoroka**
- **Okutoṣa**
- **Okutuma**
- **Okutunga**
- **Okutunguura**
- **Okutuura**
- **Okutwaara**
- **Okuvuga**
- **Okuyoomba**

- To run childishly
- To visit, to travel
- to be stable, balanced, calm or settled
- To cook
- To prepare
- To climb
- To hit, to strike
- To make noise, to shout
- To meet (in a large group)
- To take the trouble to do something
- To put in order
- To wait for
- To wait
- To chop; to be chopped
- To climb down
- To cut excess vegetation
- To meet or unite
- To meet or unite somewhere
- To buy beer for somebody
- To shake
- To fear
- To fear, to be afraid
- To hold a baby
- To escape
- To over dilute something
- To send a message via somebody
- To get, to obtain, to keep
- To develop, to raise something from the beginning
- To settle, to inhabit, to live
- To take, to deliver
- To drive, to lead, to ride (a bicycle, motorcycle, etc)
- To shout, to make noise

- **Okuzaana**
- **Okuziba**
- **Okuzibira**
- **Okuziimba**
- **Okuzina**
- **Okuzitira; okuzitiririrwa**

- **Okwaanga; okwaangwa**

- **Okwakiira**
- **Okwangana**

- **Okweeba**
- **Okweebwa**
- **Okweega**
- **Okweera**

- **Okwegoomba**

- **Okwegyesa**
- **Okwehuuta**
- **Okweita**

- **Okwekorera**
- **Okwemerera**
- **Okwemererera** (A mouthful to pronounce!)

- **Okwengyengyeta**
- **Okwerigatsa**

- **Okweshereka**
- **Okweshongora**
- **Okwesiga**
- **Okwesiga**
- **Okwesyamura**
- **Okweteekateka**
- **Okweteenga**

- To play
- To stop
- To prevent
- To swell
- To dance
- To build a fence; to have a fence built around something

- To hate, to refuse, to dislike; to be hated

- To receive
- To dislike each another, to hate one another, to divorce

- To be forgotten
- To forget
- To learn
- To ripen or be ready (for harvesting)

- To fancy oneself with something

- To teach
- To hurry
- To kill oneself, to commit suicide

- To carry on the head
- To stand
- To stand for (as in a godparent or a person who bails one out)

- To glitter, to shine
- To lick oneself, like a lion after a meal

- To hide oneself
- To sing
- To trust
- To trust, to believe in
- To sneeze
- To prepare oneself
- To need, to desire

- **Okwetegyereza**
- **Okwetoonda**
- **Okwezirika**

- To understand
- To be careful
- To wrap oneself in something; to tie oneself with something (a belt, for example); to fortify oneself against an adversary, a fight, a storm, etcetera

- **Okweziriinga**

- To move lethargically or languidly

- **Okwigara akanwa**

- To shut up! Literally, to have one's mouth plugged!

- **Okwiita**
- **Okwijura**
- **Okwijuuka**
- **Okwijuusya**
- **Okwimuka**
- **Okwiniika**
- **Okwiragura**
- **Okwiruka**
- **Okwirukana**

- To kill
- To fill, to fill up
- To remember
- To remind
- To rise
- To immerse something
- To be black, to be dark
- To run
- To have diarrhoea, literally, "to run on and on"

- **Okwombeka**
- **Okwongyera**
- **Okwonka**
- **Okwooga**
- **Okwoonsya**
- **Okwoosha**
- **Okwoosya**
- **Okwoota**

- To build
- To add to or for
- To breast-feed
- To bathe, to swim
- To breastfeed
- To miss, to be absent
- To burn, to roast, to singe
- To enjoy warmth or to be heated by a source of heat

- **Okworeka**
- **Okworoba**
- **Okwiita; okwiitwa**

- To show, to demonstrate
- To be soft, to be flexible
- To kill; to be killed

PHOTO BY EDWARD NOBEL BISAMUNYU

TO LOVE: A MUKIGA MOTHER AND CHILD
OKUKUNDA: OMWAANA NA NYINA

Chapter Eight

Affirmative and Negative
Obubaho N'obutabaho

To be and not to be!

We conjugate every verb in Lukiga and Lunyankole using the verb "to be" or "not to be" ¬ ***obubaho n' obutabaho.*** However, we also use so many contractions that one can get lost in the process of trying to explain them. Below, I will first explain the verb "to be" by showing English-Lukiga equivalents and their literal meanings. As you will see, this material will seem very familiar because we saw personal pronouns in Chapter Six.

In the subsequent section, I will give the abbreviated forms of the verb. If you have no patience with details, please learn any one of the following three sections and ignore the rest. The first one is very formal, the second one formal, and the third one informal.

Whenever my father said, **"Tindeenda!"** or **"Taawendeenda!"** or **"Taandenda!"** or some other such phrase beginning with **"Ti-",** I knew that my request had not just been denied but had been flatly denied! Generally, in Lunyankole-Lukiga, **ni-**and **-ri-**stand for is or are. However, **ti** represents the opposite. Thus, for such a short stranded word, it stands for a lot: "It is not!" For example, the Bakiga are fond of saying, **"We ti muntu!"** This sentence literally means "Him, he is not a person!" or "Her, she is not a person!" This is not to imply that a person is not human. It is a way of saying that a person is cruel or brutal and is probably equivalent to "He is an animal!" or "She is an animal!" in English. The important point here is that **ti** means is not or are not.

- I am . . .
- I am not . . .
- You are . . . (singular)
- You are not . . .
- He is . . . /She is . . .
- He is not/She is not . . .
- We are . . .
- We are not . . .
- You are . . . (plural)
- You are not . . .
- They are . . .
- They are not . . .
- It is . . .
- It is not . . .

- **Nyowe n-di** . . . ¬ Me, I am being . . .
- **Nyowe ti-ndi-**
- **Iwe o-ri** . . . ¬ You, you are being . . .
- **Iwe ti-ori** . . . ¬ (Contracts to): **Iwe t-ori**
- **We a-ri** . . . ¬ Him, he is being . . .
- **We ti-ari** . . . ¬ **We tari** . . .
- **Itwe tu-ri** . . . ¬ We, we are being . . .
- **Itwe ti-turi** . . . ¬ We, we are not being . . .
- **Imwe mu-ri** . . . ¬ You, you are being . . .
- **Imwe ti-muri** . . . ¬ You, you are not being . . .
- **Bo ba-ri** . . . ¬ Them, they are being . . .
- **Bo ti-bari** . . .
- **Yo e-ri** . . . ¬ It, it is being . . .
- **Yo teri** . . .

Clearly, getting rid of the first object pronoun address gives us a more convenient contraction. In the section above you can see that there are two types of prefixes both corresponding to one another and representing the same idea. In the following section one of them is dropped without changing the meaning of the verb.

- I am . . .
- You are . . . (singular)

- **Nyowe n-di** . . . ¬ I, I am . . .
- **Iwe o-ri** . . . ¬ You, you are . . .

- He is … /She is …
- We are …
- You are … (plural)
- They are …
- It is …

- **We a-ri** … ¬ Him, he is …
- **Itwe tu-ri** … ¬ Us, we are …
- **Imwe mu-ri** … ¬ You, you are …
- **Bo ba-ri** … ¬ Them, they are …
- **Yo e-ri** … ¬ It, it is …

In the above section we have dropped one of the prefixes and yet retained the meaning of the verb as it should be. In the following section, as I have mentioned and explained before, we will drop the pronouns because their "supporting prefixes" retain references to them.

I am …
You are … (singular)
He is … / She is …
We are …
You are … (plural)
They are …
It is …

N-di … ¬ Me, I am …
O-ri … ¬ You, you are …
A-ri … ¬ Him, he is …
Tu-ri … ¬ We are …
Mu-ri … ¬ You are …
Ba-ri … ¬ They are …
E-ri … ¬ It, it is …

STATEMENTS IN THE NEGATIVE

Generally, we make negative statements in Lukiga and Lunyankole by adding the prefix **ti-**before the pronoun prefix in an affirmative sentence. For example:

- **Nyowe, ni-mu-kuunda.**
- I, I love him. Or: I, I love her.

We can make this a negative statement by writing or saying,

- **Nyowe ti-ndi-*ku*-mukuunda.**
- I, I don't love him. Or: I, I don't love her.

Notice that a new insertion of **-*ku*-**has been made. This is because in the Present Tense of the negative form we use the infinitive form of the verb. For Example:

- **Nyowe tindikugyeenda.**
- **Nyowe tindikuhikayo.**
- **Tindikufayo!**

- I, I am not going.
- I, I will not reach.
- I don't mind. (This verb, **okufayo,** seems to have derived from the verb **okufa** or "to die".)

Review Exercise

In the following exercises, construct the affirmative or find the affirmative when the negative sentence is given.

- **We ni omuntu murungyi.)** (Contracts to ¬ **We n'omuntu murungyi.)**
- **Iwe ori omuntu w'amaani.** (Sounds as ¬ **Iwe oryomuntu murungyi.)**
- **We ni omwaana mubi.** (Contracts to ¬ **We n'omwaana mubi.)**
- **We ti mwaana mubi.**

- **Eihanga ni rirungyi.**
- **Eihanga ti rirungyi.**

- **Omupiira ni mubi.**
- **Omupiira ti mubi.**

- **Omwaana wangye ari gye.**
- **Omwaana wangye tari gye.**

- **Emeeza yeitu etebekeine.**
- **Emeeza yeitu t'etebekeine.** (This is difficult because of the repetitive **t**-sound! Contracts from **Emeeza yeitu ti etebekeine.**) See **okutebeekana** in the verbs chapter.

- **Enyonyoozi ziri hare munonga.**
- **Enyonyoozi tiziri hare munonga.**

- **Orujungu rugumire.**
- **Orujungu tirugumire.**

Affirmative statements versus their negatives ones

- I am ...
- You are ... (singular)
- He is ... /She is ...
- We are ...
- You are ... (plural)
- **Bo ti-ba-ri** ...
- It is ...

- **Nyowe ndi** ...
- **Nyowe ti-n-di** ... ¬ I, I am not being ...
- **Iwe ori** ...
- **Iwe t-o-ri** ... ¬ You, you are not being ...
- **We t-a-ri** ... ¬ Him, he is not being ...
- **Itwe ti-tu-ri** ... ¬ We, we are not being ...
- **Imwe ti-mu-ri** ... ¬ You, you are not being ...
- Them, they are not being ...
- **Yo t-e-ri** ... ¬ It, it is not being ...

All of the above can be contracted into the following forms by dropping the main pronominal parts at the beginning.

- I am ...
- You are ... (singular)
- He is ... /She is ...
- We are ...
- You are ... (plural)
- They are ...
- It is ...

- **Ti-n-di** ... ¬ Me, I am not ...
- **T-o-ri** ... ¬ You, you are not ...
- **Ta-ri** ... ¬ Him, he is not ...
- **Ti-tu-ri** ... ¬ We are not ...
- **Ti-mu-ri** ... ¬ You are not ...
- **Ti-ba-ri** ... ¬ They are not ...
- **T-e-ri** ... ¬ It, it is not ...

Practice Exercises

Many names in Lukiga are negative statements! It is a habit of Bakiga to use their sons' names either to affirm or contradict a cardinal belief. Names have been used to pre-empt curses or affirm blessings. In the following exercise I have used names that appear in Lukiga as statements and their negative forms.

- **Ndyamubona!** I will find him! (This is commonly a reference to God, or Christ.)

- **Tindimubona!** I will never find him! (This is a name but I doubt that it refers to God! Some names in Lukiga are given in reference to the difficulties encountered in begetting children.)
- **Turyamubona!** We shall find him!
- **Titurimubona!** We shall never find him! (This is not a name but it could be.)
- **Tinzaara!** I do not give birth!
- **Twinamasiko!** We have hope!
- **Titwine masiko!** ¬ We have no hope! (This is not a name.)
- **Twijukye!** ¬ Let's remember! Or: Let's not forget!
- **Titweijuka!** ¬ We do not remember!
- **Tugumisirize!** ¬ We must persevere! Or: We must be patient!
- **Tutagumisiriza!** ¬ We must not be patient! (This is not a name.)
- **Turyagyenda!** ¬ We shall go! (This is a reference to our transient state here on earth.)
- **Tituryangyeenda!** ¬ We shall not go! (This is not a name.)
- **Turyahikayo!** ¬ We shall arrive! Or: We shall reach there! (Probably a reference to the state of achieving goals.)

Chapter Nine

Conjugating Verbs
Okugeita Enkora

To conjugate a verb is to modify it so that it matches the time it is describing. In Lukiga as well as in English the modification of this verb is quite simple. For example, in English, we write a verb in its infinitive form as follows, "to speak".

It is this form that we modify to achieve the "conjugation" or "marriage" of verb and time. Let us conjugate the verb "to speak" to illustrate this in both English and Lukiga. Note the changes that take place in the Lukiga sentences to learn how verb conjugation is achieved:

To speak	Okugaamba
I will speak	**Ninyija kugaamba*** (see next row)
I will speak	**Ndaija kugaamba**
I am speaking	**Ningaamba***
I am speaking	**Ndagaamba**
I have spoken	**Nagambire**
I could have spoken	**Nkabeire ngambire**
I spoke	**Nkagaamba**
I speak	**Ngaamba**

*These forms are prevalent amongst a substantial population of the Bakiga. These forms seem to have come from the fact that **Nyowe ndi-**(Me, I am) substituted for **Nyowe ni-**.

Okurya ¬ to eat

I

SIMPLE FUTURE
Nyowe ni-nyija kurya.   Me, I will eat. Literally, this means "I will come to eat."

PRESENT PROGRESSIVE
Nyowe ni-ndya.   Me, I am eating.

PRESENT PERFECT
Nyowe na-a-rya.   Me, I have eaten.

SIMPLE PAST
Nyowe n-ka-rya.   Me, I ate.

SIMPLE PRESENT
Nyowe n-dya.   Me, I eat (always).

CONDITIONAL
We conjugate this verb by using the verb that indicates power or capacity: to be able to
Kuri nojira ngu nimbaasa nkariire.
Or: **Kuri mbasiize nkariire.**   If I could I would eat.

You

SIMPLE FUTURE
Iwe noija-kurya.   You, you will eat.

PRESENT PROGRESSIVE
Iwe noorya.   You, you are eating.

PRESENT PERFECT
Iwe waa-rya.   You, you have eaten.

SIMPLE PAST
Iwe okarya.   You, you ate.

SIMPLE PRESENT
Iwe orya.   You, you eat (always).

CONDITIONAL
Kuri nojira . . . iwe okariire. If you could, you would eat.

He/She

SIMPLE FUTURE
- **We naija kurya.**   • He [She] will eat.

PRESENT PROGRESSIVE
- **We naarya.**   • He [She] is eating.

PRESENT PERFECT
- **We yaarya.**   • He [She] has eaten.

SIMPLE PAST
- **We akarya.**   • He [She] ate.

SIMPLE PRESENT
- **We arya.**   • He [She] eats.

CONDITIONAL
- **Kuri nojira ngu nabaasa akariire.**   • If he [she] could he [she] would eat.

They

SIMPLE FUTURE
Bo nibeija kurya.   They will eat.

PRESENT PROGRESSIVE
Bo nibarya.   They are eating.

PRESENT PERFECT
Bo baarya.   They have eaten.

SIMPLE PAST
Bo bakarya.   They ate.

SIMPLE PRESENT
Bo barya.   They eat (always).

CONDITIONAL
Kuri nojira ngu nibabaasa bakariire.   If they could they would eat.

It

- **Yo neija kurya.**   It will eat.
- **Yo neerya.**   It is eating.
- **Yo yaarya.**   It has eaten.
- **Yo ekarya.**   It ate.
- **Yo erya.**   It eats.
- **Kuri nojira . . . yo ekariire.**   If it could it would eat.

Chapter Ten

REFLEXIVE INFINITIVE VERBS
ENKORA EZEGARUKIREMU

Lunyakole-Lukiga has a famous proverb, **Ekyezaara n'entare n'engwe!** It means, "It is only the lion and the leopard that produce precise images of themselves!" This, of course, is reflexive. (Presumably, all lions look alike to us but to each other the differences are glaring.)

A normal infinitive verb, as we **have** seen previously, takes the form of **oku** ... For example, **oku-gaamba.**

- **Okugaamba** ¬ to speak, to talk, to say

In some cases, the verb ends with a preposition. The suffix **-ho** represents just such a preposition in **okugaamba-ho.** In English it would mean "about" or "on". Thus, **okugaambaho** means "to speak about" or "to talk about".

As I have mentioned before, sometimes Lunyankole-Lukiga loses the **o-**prefix so that an infinitive verb is, for example, **kugaamba.** This, of course, is an exercise is saving time so that one can say something in as short a time as possible but it alters nothing.

Reflexive infinitive verbs take the same form. We can say **okwegaaamba,** or **kwegaamba.** The **-kwe-,** short as it is, stands for an action that is done unto self. Thus, we can substitute **okwe-**or

kwe- for **oku-** or **ku-** and change the meaning of a verb. So, we can go from **okugaamba** to **okwegaamba.**

Thus, **o-kwe-gaamba** means to speak about oneself. This covers all persons so that the following are possible:

As I have already explained, **okwe-** or **kwe-** is the prefix or midfix that represents "the self" in the infinitive form. However, in conjugated forms reflexive pronoun midfixes, which resemble closely their corresponding object pronouns, become operative as indicated in the following examples:

LUNYANKOLE-LUKIGA
(SHADED COLUMNS STAND FOR A VERSION OF LUKIGA SOMETIMES CALLED LUSIGYI)[6]

ENGLISH

Lunyankole-Lukiga	English
• Ninyegaambaho.	• I am speaking about myself.
• Ndegaambaho. (A variant of the above.)	• I am speaking about myself.
• Noyegaambaho.	• You are speaking about yourself.
• Oregaambaho. (A variant of the above.)	• You are speaking about yourself.
• Nayegaambaho.	• He/she is speaking about himself/herself.
• Aregaambaho. (A variant of the above.)	• He/she is speaking about himself/herself.
• Nitwegaambaho.	• We are speaking about ourselves.
• Turegaambaho. (A variant of the above.)	• We are speaking about ourselves.
• Nimwegaambaho.	• You are speaking about yourselves.
• Muregaambaho. (A variant of the above.)	• You are speaking about yourselves.

---

[6] I have only given Lusigyi, which is spoken by many other clans among the Bakiga, partial treatment in this book. However, it is a project for the fure because this language variation is completely fascinating for me. However, its total inclusion here would have made it difficult to include Lunyankole in this book's analysis.

- Nibegaambaho.
- Baregaambaho. (A variant of the above.)

- They are speaking about themselves.
- They are speaking about themselves.

For a clearer understanding of these forms it will help to study the comparison between reflexive and non-reflexive forms, as I have shown below:

LUNYANKOLE-LUKIGA

- **Ninyegaambaho.**
- **Noyegaambaho.**
- **Nayegaambaho.**
- **Nitwegaambaho.**
- **Nimwegaambaho.**
- **Nibegaambaho.**

ENGLISH

- **Ningaamba.** ¬ I am speaking.
- **Nogaamba.** ¬ You (singular) are speaking.
- **Nagaamba.** ¬ He/she is speaking.
- **Nitugaamba.** ¬ We are speaking.
- **Nimugaamba.** ¬ You (plural) are speaking.
- **Nibagaamba.** ¬ They are speaking.

FOR CLARITY, LET'S LOOK AT THE FOLLOWING ANALYSIS:

He will speak about himself.

- **O-kwe-gaamba-ho** ¬ to speak of or about oneself

Adding **-ho** to the end gives us, **okwegaambaho,** which means 'to speak about oneself'. Thus, **-ho** stands for "about" or "on" but it is really superfluous because **-kwe-**serves the same purpose. It is true to say that both should work together in formal speech but in casual speech the **-ho** is often dropped.

- **O-kwe-yaanga** ¬ to dislike oneself

Note: There are verbs which, coincidentally, begin with **O-kwe-** but are not reflexive infinitives!

- **O-kw-enda** ¬ to want
- **O-kwe-ebwa** ¬ to forget
- **O-kwetaba** ¬ to reply (when called)

In these, the midfix **-ye-** is inserted to create a reflexive infinitive.

- **Okwe-ye-enda** ¬ to want oneself, to like oneself usually better than others

In other cases, the midfixes can be terribly confusing so that one cannot tell which one represents the self and which one stands for the infinitive form of the verb. **O-kwe-ku-unda,** or to love oneself, and **okwe-ku-ngaanya,** or to gather or collect oneself, illustrate this confusion! In both cases the **-kwe-** stands for "self" and the **-ku-** represents the infinitive action or time of the verb.

A few reflexive verbs:

- **Okweshusha** • To look like oneself ¬ often used about a parent whose son or daughter is their exact copy
- **Okwehana** • To berate oneself
- **Okwekurura** • To be very slow in one's habits
- **Okwetamwa** • To be bored by one's own company
- **Okwerundarunda** • To pull oneself together, to recover

Chapter Eleven

THE PEOPLE (OMU-ABA) GROUP
OMUGABO GWABAANTU (OMU-ABA)

Nouns, in Lunyankole-Lukiga, exist in what one might call "noun groups". Each group consists of two sub-groups, the singular and the plural. From a particular prefix in the name of an object or a person one can tell the groups to which a noun belongs. Why is this important? In the same way French determines that nouns are masculine or feminine many rules of grammar, as we shall see later, depend on these classifications.

Noun Groups

The Human Group or the People Group
[Omu-/Aba-Group]

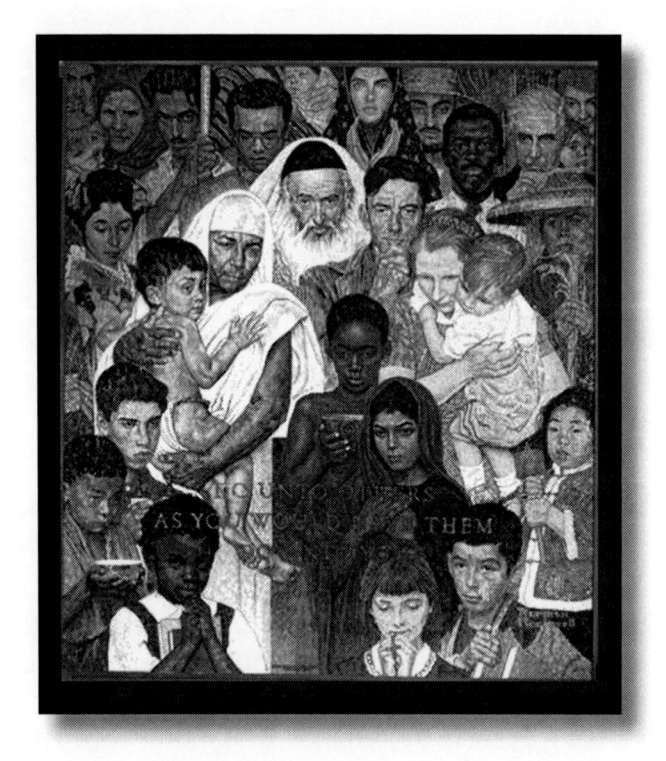

A Painting by Norman Rockwell, an American Artist
**Ekishushaani ekyateirwe omukugu waabyo kandi omunyaamerika,
Norman Rockwell**

The People Group has the prefix **Omu-** for singular and **Aba-** for plural. For example, **omuntu** stands for "a person" while **abantu** stands for "people". By looking at the root word **"-ntu"** we can recognise the main clue for a name of a person or people. It is really the prefixes that give us an idea of how many people are involved. However, it should also be borne in mind, from the beginning, that even though "a thing" or "things" belong to another class, in Lunyankole-Lukiga, their name is derived from the same root as that which describes people. This is not surprising because a thing or things are implements or tools people use so the two nouns, people and things, are closely related. As I will show in their respective noun group in a later Chapter, we tell them apart from people by the prefix that defines their group.

Noun in Lunyankole-Lukiga

- **Omu-ntu**[7]
- **Aba-ntu**
- **Omujungu**
- **Abajungu**
- **Omukiga**
- **Abakiga**
- **Omwoojo (from Omu-oojo)**
- **Aboojo (from Aba-oojo)**
- **Omujirimani**
- **Abajirimani**
- **Omurachi**
- **Abarachi**
- **Omuhindi**
- **Abahindi**
- **Omuharabu**
- **Abaharabu**
- **Omushomesa**
- **Abashomesa**
- **Omwaami**
- **Abaami**

Noun in English

- a person
- persons/people
- a European
- Europeans
- a Kiga person
- Kiga people
- a boy
- Boys
- A German
- Germans
- Dutch person
- Dutch people
- an Indian
- Indians
- an Arab
- Arabs
- a teacher
- Teachers
- a lord, a chief
- lords, chiefs

---

[7] You have heard of the Bantu people of East, Central, and Southern Africa. Their languages, which differ widely, belong to the Bantu linguistic class. Languages in this class have at least the word for PERSON in common: **Omuntu,** or its plural form **Abantu,** has many variations. **Muntu/bantu,** or **umuntu/abantu** and others all refer to the same noun. It is interesting to note also that "things" have the same root as "people" even if the prefix is different. For example: **eki-ntu/ebi-ntu**. We will see more nouns from this group later but it is apparent from this that "things" or "property" derive their name from the name for "people".

PHOTO BY THE AUTHOR'S GODMOTHER, LILIAN CLARKE

A COLONIAL AFRICAN CHIEF
OMWAAMI OMU BAAMI!

While such terms as **omujungu** and **omurachi** may refer to the generic singular for both male and female, a special suffix, **-kazi**[8], is often used for females. For example:

- **Omujungu-kazi** ¬ a European woman
- **Abajungu-kazi** ¬ European women

- **Omukigakazi** ¬ a Mukiga woman
- **Abakigakazi** ¬ Bakiga women

- **Omujirimanikazi** ¬ a German woman
- **Abajirimanikazi** ¬ German women

- **Omunyankolekazi** ¬ an Ankole woman
- **Abanyankolekazi** ¬ Ankole women

---

[8] The suffix **-kazi** may refer to a woman or to the wife of the person to whose name it is attached. For example ¬ **Omuhindi-kazi** may refer to an Indian woman or to a wife of an Indian man.

- **Omuharabukazi** ¬ an Arab woman
- **Abaharabukazi** ¬ Arab women

- **Omuhindikazi** ¬ An Indian woman
- **Abahindikazi** ¬ Indian women

- **Omugandakazi** ¬ a Muganda woman
- **Abagandakazi** ¬ Baganda women

- **Omushomesakazi** ¬ a female teacher
- **Abashomesakazi** ¬ female teachers

- **Omunywaani** ¬ a friend
- **Abanywaani** ¬ friends: This, in my view, is one of the most interesting nouns we have in Lunyankole-Lukiga. It seems to have been derived from the verb *to drink*, or, **okunywa!** This should not surprise one at all because I have never seen a society that takes drinking more seriously than that in Kigezi! Given that a friend is often invited to a drink, the word **omunywaani,** naturally, means *one with whom you drink* and yet, friend, as well! Literally, fellow drunks are called friends!

POSSESSIVE PRONOUNS FOR THE **OMU-ABA** NOUN GROUP

EXAMPLE 1

1ST PERSON SINGULAR

- **Omwaana waangye** • My child
- **Abaana baangye** • My children

2ⁿᵈ PERSON SINGULAR

- **Omwaana waawe**
- **Abaana baawe**

- Your child
- Your children

3ʳᵈ PERSON SINGULAR

- **Omwaana weeye**
- **Abaana beeye**

- His/her child
- His/her children

1ˢᵗ PERSON PLURAL

- **Omwaana weitu**
- **Abaana beitu**

- Our child
- Our children

2ⁿᵈ PERSON PLURAL

- **Omwaana waanyu**
- **Abaana baanyu**

- Your child
- Your children

3ʳᵈ PERSON PLURAL

- **Omwaana waabo**
- **Abaana baabo**

- Their child
- Their children

PHOTO BY EDWARD NOBEL BISAMUNYU

FRIENDS
ABANYWAANI

Chapter Twelve

THE EKI-EBI NOUN GROUP
OMUGABO GWA EKI-EBI

This group includes one of the most extensive collections of nouns. Its singular form begins with **eki-** and its plural form with **ebi-,** as the following list shows:

LUKIGA	ENGLISH
• **Ekitabo/Ebitabo**	• A book/books
• **Ekibi/Ebibi**	• A sin/sins
• **Ekihuguhugu/ Ebihuguhugu**	• A butterfly/butterflies
• **Ekirunda/Ebirunda**	• A wound/wounds
• **Ekitigu/Ebitigu**	• A liver/livers
• **Ekyoozi/Ebyoozi**	• A pumpkin/pumpkins
• **Ekibaanja/Ebibaanja**	• A plot of land/plots of land
• **Ekiju/Ebiju**	• A big house/big houses
• **Ekitakuri/Ebitakuri**	• A sweet potato/sweet potatoes
• **Ekihorooni/Ebihorooni**	• A latrine/latrines
• **Ekikaari/Ebikaari**	• A backyard/backyards

POSSESSIVE PRONOUNS FOR THE EKI-EBI NOUN GROUP

*IN THIS GROUP, THE NOUN BEGINS WITH **EKI-**IN ITS SINGULAR FORM AND **EBI-**IN ITS PLURAL FORM*

Example 1

1ˢᵗ Person Singular

- **Ekitabo kyangye**
- **Ebitabo byangye**

- My book
- My books

2ⁿᵈ Person Singular

- **Ekitabo kyaangye**
- **Ebitabo byaangye**

- Your book
- Your books

3ʳᵈ Person Singular

- **Ekitabo kyeeye**
- **Ebitabo byeeye**

- His/her book
- His/her books

1ˢᵗ Person Plural

- **Ekitabo kyeitu**
- **Ebitabo byeitu**

- Our book
- Our books

2ⁿᵈ Person Plural

- **Ekitabo kyaanyu**
- **Ebitabo byaanyu**

- Your book
- Your books

3ʳᵈ Person Plural

- **Ekitabo kyaabo**
- **Ebitabo byaabo**

- Their book
- Their books

Example 2

1ˢᵗ Person Singular

- **Ekibaanja kyaangye**
- **Ebibaanja byaangye**

- My plot of land
- My plots of land

2ⁿᵈ Person Singular

- **Ekibaanja kyaawe** — Your plot of land
- **Ebibaanja byaawe** — Your plots of land

3ʳᵈ Person Singular

- **Ekibaanja kyeeye** — His/her plot of land
- **Ebibaanja byeeye** — His/her plots of land

1ˢᵗ Person Plural

- **Ekibaanja kyeitu** — Our plot of land
- **Ebibaanja byeitu** — Our plots of land

2ⁿᵈ Person Plural

- **Ekibaanja kyaanyu** — Your plot of land
- **Ebibaanja byaanyu** — Your plots of land

3ʳᵈ Person Plural

- **Ekibaanja kyaabo** — Their plot of land
- **Ebibaanja byaabo** — Their plots of land

Chapter Thirteen

THE E-AMA NOUN GROUP
OMUGABO GWA E-AMA

The E-Ama Group has the prefix **e-**for nouns in singular form and **ama-**for the plural form. Therefore, we derive the name E-Ama Noun Group from these prefixes. For example, **eihuri** means "an egg" and **amahuri** mean "eggs". The root for **eihuri, -huri,** denotes "egg" while the different prefixes tell us the number of items in question.

PHOTO BY EDWARD NOBEL BISAMUNYU

A CHURCH IN SODERMALM, STOCKHOLM
EKANISA OMURI SODERMALM, STOCKHOLM

LUKIGA	ENGLISH
• **Eibeere, amabeere**	• A breast, breasts
• **Eibega, amabega**	• A shoulder, shoulders
• **Eichumu, amachumu**	• A spear, spears
• **Eihangwe, amahangwe**	• An evening, evenings
• **Eihega, amahega**	• A hearthstone, hearthstones
• **Eihuri, amahuri**	• An egg, eggs
• **Eihwa, amahwa**	• A thorn, thorns
• **Eirebe, amarebe**	• Water lily, water lilies
• **Eirwariro, amarwariro**	• A hospital, hospitals
• **Eishaza, amashaza**	• A pea, peas
• **Eishaza,[9] amashaza**	• A county, counties
• **Eishomero, amashomero**	• A school, schools
• **Eitako, amatako**	• A pelvic bone, pelvic bones
• **Eitama, amatama**	• A cheek, cheeks
• **Eitembero, amatembero**	• A stair or a step, stairs or steps
• **Eiyasha, amayasha**	• A loin, loins
• **Ekanisa, amakanisa**	• A church, churches
• **Enju, amaju**	• A house, houses
• **Eriisho, amaisho**	• An eye, eyes
• **Eryanda, Amanda**	• A battery cell, battery cells

---

[9] Derived from Luganda. A saza was a county in the old Kingdom of Buganda, and was led by a saza chief. British colonial rule, using Bugandan administration personnel and techniques, adopted saza counties all over Uganda. For the Bakiga and Banyankole the word must have sounded like peas! However, it could just as easily have been obtained from Lukiga, where okushar**a means** to *cut or to divide. Thus, literally, eishaza means a division!*

PHOTO BY EDWARD NOBEL BISAMUNYU

A HOUSE, HOUSES
ENJU, AMAJU

POSSESSIVE PRONOUNS FOR THE *E-A* NOUN GROUP

EXAMPLE 1

1ST PERSON SINGULAR

- **Enju yangye**
- **Amaju gaangye**

- My house
- My houses

2ND PERSON SINGULAR

- **Enju yaawe**
- **Amaju gaawe**

- Your house
- Your houses

3RD PERSON SINGULAR

- **Enju yeeye**
- **Amaju geeye**

- His/her house
- His/her houses

1ˢᵀ PERSON PLURAL

- **Enju yeitu**
- **Amaju geitu**

- Our house
- Our houses

2ᴺᴰ PERSON PLURAL

- **Enju yaanyu**
- **Amaju gaanyu**

- Your house
- Your houses

3ᴿᴰ PERSON PLURAL

- **Enju yaabo**
- **Amaju gaabo**

- Their house
- Their houses

NOTE ¬

Some nouns, such as **eihuri/amahuri** (egg/eggs), **eryanda/amanda** (a battery cell/battery cells), **eihwa/amahwa** (a thorn/thorns) and others in the **E-Ama** Noun Group, however, take a slightly different possessive prefix in the singular form:

1ˢᵀ PERSON SINGULAR

- **Eihuri ryangye**
- **Amahuri gangye**

- My egg
- My eggs

2ᴺᴰ PERSON SINGULAR

- **Eihuri ryaawe**
- **Amahuri gaawe**

- Your egg
- Your eggs

3ᴿᴰ PERSON SINGULAR

- **Eihuri ryeeye**
- **Amahuri geeye**

- His/her egg
- His/her eggs

1ˢᵀ PERSON PLURAL

- **Eihuri ryeitu**
- **Amahuri geitu**

- Our egg
- Our eggs

2ᴺᴰ Person Plural

- **Eihuri ryaanyu**
- **Amahuri gaanyu**

- Your egg
- Your eggs

3ᴿᴰ Person Plural

- **Eihuri ryaabo**
- **Amahuri gaabo**

- Their egg
- Their eggs

Chapter Fourteen

THE OMU-EMI NOUN GROUP
OMUGABO GWA OMU-EMI

PHOTO BY EDWARD NOBEL BISAMUNYU

THE BACK!
OMUGONGO!

The **Omu-Emi** Group has the prefix **omu-**for nouns in their singular form and **emi-**for the plural form. Again, we have derived the name of the group from its relevant prefixes. The word **omugongo** stands for *a back* and **emigongo** for *backs.* The root **-gongo** then denotes back, while the prefixes tell us that it is singular or plural.

Lukiga

- **Omugongo/emigongo**
- **Omukono/emikono**
- **Omunwa/eminwa**
- **Omuryo/emiryo**

- **Omuṣhozi/emiṣhozi**
- **Omutwe/emitwe**
- **Omutwe/emitwe**
- **Omuze/emize**
- **Omuzi/emizi**
- **Omurabyo/emirabyo**
- **Omuṣerebende/ emiṣerebende**
- **Omurundi/emirundi**
- **Omurundi/emirundi**
- **Omugaanda/emigaanda**
- **Omuguha/emiguha**
- **Omweenda/emyeenda**

- **Omuhoro/emihoro**
- **Omupiira/emipiira**
- **Omuriro/emiriro**
- **Omuze/emize**
- **Omuzi/emizi**
- **Omuti/emiti**
- **Omutumba**[10]**/emitumba**

English

A back/backs
An arm/arms
A mouth/mouths
A method/methods ¬ The word omuryo probably comes from the verb to eat (okurya). Literally, a way of eating.

A hill/hills
A head/ heads
A plan/plans
A habit/habits
A root/roots
A lightning/lightning(s)
A limousine/limousines

A time/times
A tibia/tibias (a bone in the leg)
A bundle/bundles
A rope/ropes
A piece of cloth or clothing/pieces of cloth or clothing

A sickle/sickles
A ball/balls
A fire/fires
A habit/habits
A root/roots
A tree/trees
A banana tree/banana trees

---

[10] Not to be confused with omutu**mbi and emit**umbi, which mean "corpse" and "corpses", respectively.

Photo: Edward Nobel Bisamunyu

Rugarama Hill overlooking Bubaare, Kigezi
Ahamushozi gwa Rugarama orikuraanzya Bubaare, Kigezi

Possessive pronouns for the **OMU-EMI** noun group

Example 1

1ST Person Singular

- **Omuguha gwangye**
- **Emiguha yangye**

- My rope
- My ropes

2ND Person Singular

- **Omuguha gwaawe**
- **Emiguha yaawe**

- Your rope
- Your ropes

3RD Person Singular

- **Omuguha gweeye**
- **Emiguha yeeye**

- His/her rope
- His/her ropes

1ˢᵗ Person Plural

- **Omuguha gweitu**
- **Emiguha yeitu**

- Our rope
- Our ropes

2ⁿᵈ Person Plural

- **Omuguha gwaanyu**
- **Emiguha yanyu**

- Your rope
- Your ropes

3ʳᵈ Person Plural

- **Omuguha gwaabo**
- **Emiguha yaabo**

- Their rope
- Their ropes

Example 2

1ˢᵗ Person Singular

- **Omutwe gwaangye**
- **Emitwe yaangye**

- My head
- My heads

2ⁿᵈ Person Singular

- **Omutwe gwaawe**
- **Emitwe yaawe**

- Your head
- Your heads

3ʳᵈ Person Singular

- **Omutwe gweeye**
- **Emitwe yeeye**

- His/her head
- His/her heads

1ˢᵗ Person Plural

- **Omutwe gweeitu**
- **Emitwe yeeitu**

- Our head
- Our heads

2ⁿᵈ Person Plural

- **Omutwe gwaanyu**
- **Emitwe yaanyu**

- Your head
- Your heads

3ʳᵈ Person Plural

- **Omutwe gwaabo**
- **Emitwe yaabo**

- Their head
- Their heads

Chapter Fifteen

THE OKU-AMA NOUN GROUP
OMUGABO GWA OKU-AMA

The **Oku-Ama** Group includes nouns that are largely names of parts of the body! The prefix **oku-**begins the names of nouns in their singular but is modifies to **ama-**for nouns in their plural form. As there are a few nouns in this group, I have kept its list short. However, in a later Chapter, I will give a comprehensive list of names of parts of the body, which, as we shall see, includes names from every possible Noun Group.

LUKIGA	ENGLISH

- **Okuguru/amaguru**   A leg/legs
- **Okuju/amaju**   A knee/knees
- **Okutu/amatu**   An ear/ears

POSSESSIVE PRONOUNS FOR THE OKU-AMA NOUN GROUP

EXAMPLE 1

1ST PERSON SINGULAR

- **Okuguru kwaangye**   • My leg
- **Amaguru gaangye**   • My legs

2ND PERSON SINGULAR

- **Okuguru kwaawe**
- **Amaguru gaawe**

- Your leg
- Your legs

3RD PERSON SINGULAR

- **Okuguru kweeye**
- **Amaguru geeye**

- His/her leg
- His/her legs

1ST PERSON PLURAL

- **Okuguru kweitu**
- **Amaguru geitu**

- Our leg
- Our legs

2ND PERSON PLURAL

- **Okuguru kwaanyu**
- **Amaguru ganyu**

- Your leg
- Your legs

3RD PERSON PLURAL

- **Okuguru kwaabo**
- **Amaguru gaabo**

- Their leg
- Their legs

EXAMPLE 2

1ST PERSON SINGULAR

- **Okutu kwaangye**
- **Amatu gaangye**

- My ear
- My ears

2ND PERSON SINGULAR

- **Okutu kwaawe**
- **Amatu gaawe**

- Your ear
- Your ears

3RD PERSON SINGULAR

- **Okutu kweeye**
- **Amatu geeye**

- His/her ear
- His/her ears

1ˢᵀ Person Plural

- **Okutu kweeitu**
- **Amatu geeitu**

- Our ear
- Our ears

2ᴺᴰ Person Plural

- **Okutu kwaanyu**
- **Amatu gaanyu**

- Your ear
- Your ears

3ᴿᴰ Person Plural

- **Okutu kwaabo**
- **Amatu gaabo**

- Their ear
- Their ears

Chapter Sixteen

THE EM-EM/EN-EN NOUN GROUP
OMUGABO GWA EM-EM/EN-EN

PHOTO BY EDWARD NOBEL BISAMUNYU

CHICKEN/CHICKENS
ENKOKO (SINGULAR)/**ENKOKO** (PLURAL)

This group will occasionally include people and some animals but is generally a group of inanimate objects. It will be easy to see that, in this group, a person's name derives from a caricature or unflattering role or position. However, it may also derive from a person gaining a name that derives from a metaphor or simile, compared with such a noun as a shield, or a lion, or a cow!

Untenable and unfathomable in the ancient history of Kigezi was the role of a king. Unlike Buganda, Bunyoro, Toro and, just next to us,

Ankole, Kigezi was much too egalitarian to allow the ascendancy of an individual to a position of lordship. However, in our recent British colonial history, the equivalent of a king, **Rutakirwa Engabo ya Kigezi,** or the Unsurpassable and Shield of Kigezi, was installed.

One must give credit to the British colonial authorities of the time for doing their homework. Consultation with Bakiga elders must have taken place before a determination of the name to use for this office was made. It is certainly the sort of name by which even Bakiga would have been charmed into accepting a king!

Interestingly enough, in the Kingdom of Ankole where Lunyankole is spoken, a man named **Ntare**, whose name derived from **entare**, or a lion, was **Omugabe"**, or the Giver (of all things), or the King, when Captain Frederick Dealtry Lugard arrived there in the latter part of the 19th Century to thresh out an agreement with him bringing the Kingdom of Ankole under British protection.

Both **engabo** and **entare** belong to the E-E Noun Group. Thus, in both singular and plural forms **engabo** is **engabo** and **entare** is **entare.** Some of the nouns in this group, however, are uncountable and are, therefore, treated in the singular form only even though one would never know it.

LUKIGA | ENGLISH

- **Embwa/embwa** — A dog/dogs
- **Endeeba/endeeba** — A look/looks
- **Engabo/engabo** — A shield/shields
- **Engaro/engaro** — A hand/hands
- **Enkuumba/enkuumba** — A woman who cannot conceive

---

[11] Even though traditional kingdoms have been nominally restored in Uganda, the ancient Kingdom of Ankole has been denied that privilege. It is quite clear that President Yoweri Museveni, one of Africa's most prominent authors of totalitarianism, a Munyankole, sees himself as an automatic choice for that role. Thus, the hereditary king of Ankole has been kept out of the loop.

- **Enkuundwakazi/ enkundwakazi** — The favourite wife (in a polygamous household)
- **Enoono/enoono** — A heel/heels
- **Entabire/entabire** — A row (in a garden)/rows (in a garden[12])
- **Enyuungu/enyuungu** — A pot/pots
- **Enshoboroora/ enshoboroora** — An explanation/Explanations

POSSESSIVE PRONOUNS FOR THE **EM-M/EN-EN** NOUN GROUP

*In this group, the noun, in both its singular and plural forms, begins with **EM-** or **EN-**.*

EXAMPLE 1

1ST PERSON SINGULAR

- **Entabire yangye** — My gardening row
- **Entabire zangye** — My gardening rows

2ND PERSON SINGULAR

- **Entabire yaawe** — Your gardening row
- **Entabire zaawe** — Your gardening rows

3RD PERSON SINGULAR

- **Entabire yeeye** — His/her gardening row
- **Entabire zeeye** — His/her gardening rows

1ST PERSON PLURAL

- **Entabire yeitu** — Our gardening row
- **Entabire zeitu** — Our gardening rows

---

[12] In certain gardens, some food crops are sown or planted in raised rows to enable them to drain properly. Sweet potato gardens in Kigezi provide a good example.

2ⁿᴰ Person Plural

- **Entabire yaanyu**
- **Entabire zaanyu**

- Your gardening row
- Your gardening rows

3ᴿᴰ Person Plural

- **Entabire yaabo**
- **Entabire zaabo**

- Their gardening row
- Their gardening rows

Example 2

1ˢᵀ Person Singular

- **Engaro yangye**
- **Engaro zangye**

- My hand
- My hands

2ⁿᴰ Person Singular

- **Engaro yaawe**
- **Engaro zaawe**

- Your hand
- Your hands

3ᴿᴰ Person Singular

- **Engaro yeeye**
- **Engaro zeeye**

- His/her hand
- His/her hands

1ˢᵀ Person Plural

- **Engaro yeitu**
- **Engaro zeitu**

- Our hand
- Our hands

2ⁿᴰ Person Plural

- **Engaro yaanyu**
- **Engaro zaanyu**

- Your hand
- Your hands

3ᴿᴰ Person Plural

- **Engaro yaabo**
- **Engaro zaabo**

- Their hand
- Their hands

Photo by Edward Nobel Bisamunyu

My bead/My beads
Enkwaanzi yaangye/enkwaanzi zaangye

Chapter Seventeen

The Miscellaneous Nouns
Emigabo Eyemiringo

The O-Group

- **Orwaamba** — Blood from livestock, which is cooked and eaten. Blood is largely protein so it is denatured by heat and coagulates to form an edible, meaty substance, which is much the same as blood pudding in Britain. A similar blood food is also common in China.
- **Orwaari** — Noise
- **Orwaanju** — Naughtiness
- **Orwaango** — Hatred
- **Orwambiza** — Anarchy, chaos, a mess

- The possessive prefix for this group is **rw-**. For example, **orwaamba rwangye, orwaamba rwaabo.**

The Ama-Group

- **Amaani** — Power, ability, health
- **Amakara** — Charcoal, coal

- **Amaryo**
- **Amashe**
- **Amate**
- **Amaarwa**
- **Amatooto**
- **Amazi**
- **Amaizi**

- Arrogance
- Cow dung
- Milk
- Beer
- Chicken faeces
- Faeces
- Water

The possessive prefix for this group is **g-**. For example, **amaizi gaabo, amaizi geitu.**

The Abusive Groups

Other interesting noun groups exist in Lunyankole Lukiga. These groups may include nouns from other groups but in diminutive or abusive [my word] forms.

We have, for example, a book, or **ekitabo,** from the **Eki-Ebi** Group. In this form the book is considered to be a normal sized item. However, In Lunyankole Lukiga, we can diminish its size by using special prefixes from the **Aka-Obu** Group. Thus, if we call it **akatabo** instead of **ekitabo** then we have reduced its size. In plural form this would be **obutabo.** We can speak of this book as follows:

In singular form:

Akatabo kangye karungyi nakagura.

In plural form:

Obutabo bwangye burungyi nabugura.

For uncountable items, we can apply the prefix **Aka-** or **Otu-**:

- **Akashagama**
- **Otute**
- **Otwoondo**
- **Akoondo**

- A little blood
- A little milk
- A little mud
- A little mud

In addition, we can apply the **Eki-Ebi** Noun Group prefixes to enhance the size of something in speech!

Thus, we can make **embwa,** or a dog, which belongs to the **E-E** Noun Group, a much larger dog by calling it **ekibwa.** Many of them, of course, would be **ebibwa.**

Better still, we can attach prefixes from the **O-**Noun Group and make it an even bigger dog! Hence, **orubwa.**[13]

Let's make a sentence: **Orubwa rukuzire munonga.** This means, "The big dog is overgrown".

---

[13] Incidentally, **orubwa** is also a word that, as in English, means nasty doggedness or persistent botheration. As in English, it is derived from the nature of the animal it represents and infers a hunting instinct and persistence.

Chapter Eighteen

The Imported Nouns
Amaziina Gaheeru

Lunyankole Lukiga	English	Original Name	Original Language
Burangiti	Blanket	**Blanket**	English: probably introduced into both Lunyankole and Lukiga through corruption of the English word *blanket*
Ebaafu	Bath	**Bath**	English, probably via Luganda
Ebeeseni	Basin, tub	**Basin**	English: probably adopted through Luganda

Eitegura	Tile	**Tegula** ¬ This seems to have been derived from the name of a protective structure found on snails (gastropods), which acts as a roof.	Latin
Ekarayi, ekarahi	A deep metallic, basin-like vessel used for washing.	**Karai** ¬ A wok-like vessel used for frying in India.	Hindi
Ekihoroni	Toilet	**Choo** ¬ Chooni means "in the toilet".	This word must have been derived from Swahili because it recalls "chooni"
Ekikapu	Bag	**Kikapu**	Swahili: probably derived from the word kikapu, which, in Swahili, means the same thing.
Ekikopo	Cup	**Kikombe**	Swahili
Ekitabo	Book	**Kitab**	Arabic, probably via Swahili.

Emeeza	Table	**Mesa** ¬ This has also been used to describe a plateau, or a high tableland.	Latin
Emotoka	English	**Motor-car**	Corruption of the word motor-car
Enanaasi	Pineapple	**Ananas comosus** ¬ Even though this is a Latin name it derives from the word "nana", which Christopher Columbus found in the Caribbean, where the fruit was first found by his party in 1493.	Latin
Esaabuuni	Soap	**Sabuni**	Arabic, probably via Swahili and Luganda.
Esafuriya	Saucepan	**Sufuria**	Arabic, probably via Swahili.
Esande	Sunday	**Sunday**	English, probably via Luganda.

Kabada	Cupboard	**Cupboard**	English, probably via Luganda.
Misa	A service mass in church	**Missa** ¬ The most famous name that is related to this is Beethoven's *Missa solemnis,* or the "Solemn Mass", or "Requiem Service Mass".	Latin
Omudumu, sometimes this word slips into **omurumo**	Jug	**Mdomo** ¬ This word means a mouth in Swahili. The jug then appears to have been named after its lippy appearance in Lunyankole and Lukiga.	Swahili
Orupapura	Paper	**Paper** ¬ Even though "paper" is derived from "papyrus", our name for "paper" comes from English.	English

Pamba	Cotton	**Pamba**	Arabic, probably via Swahili and Luganda.
Sukaari	Sugar	**Sucre**	French

Chapter Nineteen

PARTS OF THE HUMAN BODY
EBICHWEEKA BYOMUBIRI

UGANDA ARGUS

JOHN AKII-BUA, OLYMPIC GOLD MEDALIST, (1972) IN MUNICH, GERMANY, WHO TRAINED STRENUOUSLY IN OUR HILLS IN KIGEZI

JOHN AKII-BUA, OWATUNGIRE EZAABU OMUMWAKA GWA 1972 OMURI MUNICH, GERMANY KANDI OWABEIRE NAYEGYEZAMU MUNONGA OMUMISHOZI YEITU YA KIGEZI

Parts of the human body! *Warning!* It is very rare indeed for Bakiga to name the reproductive parts of the body. These body parts are often named or discussed with the typical accompaniment of laughter and a heavy dose of shame. Decades of exposure in the field of biology, however, have dispensed with my own innate shame.

- Abdomen/abdomens
- Arm/arms ¬
- Armpit
- Back of the head
- Back/backs
- Bone/bones
- Breast/breasts
- Cheek/cheeks
- Chest/chests
- Chin/chins
- Eye/eyes
- Finger/fingers

- **enda/enda**[14]
- **omukono/emikono**
- **Okwaahwa**
- **Enkomo**
- **omugoongo/emigoongo**
- **eigufa/amagufa**
- **eibeere/amabeere**
- **eitama/amatama**
- **ekifuba/ebifuba**
- **ekireju/ebireju**
- **eriisho/ameisho**
- **ekikumu/ebikumu** or **orukumu/enkumu** or **ekyaara/ebyaara** (see below)

- Fingernail/fingernails
- Flesh
- Foot/feet
- Forehead/foreheads
- Grey hair
- Gum/gums
- Hair
- Hand/hands
- Head/heads
- Knee/knees
- Left arm
- Left hand
- Leg/legs
- Lip/lips

- **ekyaara/ebyaara**
- **enyama/enyama**
- **ekigyere/ebigyere**
- **obuso/obuso**
- **enju**[15]
- **engino/engine**
- **Eishokye**
- **engaro/engaro**
- **omutwe/emitwe**
- **okuju/amaju**
- **omukono gwa bumosho**
- **engaro ya bumosho**
- **okuguru/amaguru**
- **omunwa/eminwa**

---

[14] The words enda *and enda also refer to a louse and lice respectively!*
[15] Unfortunately, the word enju also stands for a ho*use!*

- Mouth (inside)
- Mouth (outside)
- Neck/necks
- Nose/noses
- Right arm
- Right hand
- Sheen/sheens
- Shoulder/shoulders
- Skin (not normally countable)
- Thigh/thighs
- Toe/toes
- Tongue/tongues
- Tooth/teeth

- **Akanwa**
- **omunwa/eminwa**
- **ebisya/ebisya**
- **enyiindo/enyiindo**
- **omukono gwa buryo**
- **engaro ya buryo**
- **omurundi/emirundi**
- **eibega/amabega**
- **Omubiri**

- **eitako/amatako**
- **ekyaara/ebyaara**
  - **orurimi/endimi**[16]
  - **eriino/ameino**

Photo by Edward Nobel Bisamunyu

Mr Ezrah Mulera and Mrs Irene Bisamunyu
Omwaami Ezrah Mulera n'omukyaara Irene Bisamunyu
True Bakiga dancing away at Kasooni Church, Mparo, where the eagle flies but without a place to perch because it's spoilt for choice!
Abakiga kashushu nibakisooma aha kanisa ya Kasooni, Mparo, evi empungu ezereera ekaburwa n'obugweero!

---

[16] As in English, the word tongue also stands *for language*. Thus, *orurimi* and *endimi* mean language and languages respectively.

Chapter Twenty

OUR TENSES
OBWIIRE

TENSE	ENGLISH	LUKIGA
SIMPLE PRESENT	I play.	**Nzaana.**
PRESENT CONTINUOUS	I am playing.	**Nkweise ninzaana.**
PRESENT PERFECT	I have played.	**Naaba nazaanire.**
SIMPLE PAST	I played.	**Nkazaana.**
IMPERFECT	I used to play.	**Nkaba nzaana.**
PAST CONTINUOUS	I was playing.	**Nkaba ningyeenda.**
CONDITIONAL	I would play.	**Kuri nogyira . . . nkazaanire.**
PAST PERFECT	I had played.	**Nkaba nazaanire.**
FUTURE	I shall play.	**Ninyija kuzaana.**
FUTURE PERFECT	I shall have played.	**Ndyaaba nazaanire./ Naanazanire.**
IMPERATIVE	Play!	**Zaana!**

EXPLAINING TENSES

PRESENT SIMPLE	I play.	**Nzaana.**

The **N-**in the sentence **Nzaana** is a subject pronoun and it stands for *I*, giving us *I play*. If we replaced the **N-**with **A-**then we would have **Azaana**, which means *You play*. This means that the suffix **-zaana** stands for "play". This same simple "play" gives us the imperative form, "Play!" Around this suffix, then, we can build sentences or statements in different tenses. The imperative form, for example, is **Zaana!** ¬ Play!

Present continuous   I am playing.   **Nkweise ninzaana.**

"I am playing" takes the form **Nkweise ninzaana.** We construct this sentence with the help of the verb "to hold" because, in Lukiga, everything in the Present Continuous uses this verb. So, to say anything in this tense we must attach the Present Continuous form suffix of the verb **okukwaasa,** which is **-kweise,** to the same "person" that is the subject of the sentence. To this suffix we add the relevant personal prefix, which is **N-**in this case to obtain **Nkweise.** The suffix **-kweise** simply infers that something is ongoing or, more literally, "holding".

The verb "to play", or, **okuzaana,** gives us the suffix **-zaana,** which is actually the core verb of the sentence with which we are concerned. Since we know that our sentence here is about the First Person Singular we prefix **-zaana** with another **n-**to correspond to the first **N-**we started with in front of-**kweise.** In **Nkweise ninzaana** above we have an **"n-",** which denotes "I", the First Person Singular in both verb suffixes. If we replaced this with "tu-", it would change the meaning of the sentence so that we have **Tukweise nitugyeenda.**

Present perfect   I have played.   **Naaba nazaanire.**

Again, the suffix **-zaana** plays a central role except that in this case it is modified on both ends. Firstly, the Present Perfect Tense is presented by the verb "to be", or, **okuba.** We achieve that by joining to the Present Continuous suffix **-ba** the relevant person. In this case, "I" for the First Person Singular in the form of **N-,** the prefix that is commonly fitted in front of **-ba** for First Person Singular.

However, **N-**is followed by the letter **-a-,** which infers the Present Perfect form and corresponds to the **-a-**before **-zaan-.** After the suffix **-zaan-,** we add what one might call **-ire,** which emphasises the fact that theaction we are discussing has already taken place. The suffix **-ire** seems to be an adaption of the word **ira,** which means "of old" or "long ago".

| Simple Past | I played. | **Nkazaana.** |

The lone and crucial indicator of the fact that a verb has been conjugated in the Simple Past form is **-ka-.** You may remember it by associating it with the word **kare,** which means "a long time ago".

| Imperfect | I used to play. | **Nkaba nzaana.** |

The Imperfect Tense uses the Simple Past form of the verb "to be", **okuba,** to conjugate the verb.

| Future Progressive | This time tomorrow I will be playing! | **Nkezishaha nyenkyakare ninyija kuba ninzaana.** |

| Future Perfect | This time next year I will have been playing for seven years! | **Nkezishaha omwaaka ogurikwiija ninyija kuba nabeire ninzaana kumara emyaaka mushaanju.** |

Chapter Twenty-One

THE FUTURE TENSE
EBIRYAKORWA

PHOTO BY EDWARD NOBEL BISAMUNYU

THE FUTURE
EBIRO BY'OMUMEISHO

In Lukiga the Future Tense is conjugated with the help of the verb "to come", **Okwiija,** while also retaining the infinitive form of the functional verb so that it has, at the beginning, the feature **oku-**that makes a verb infinitive becomes **ku-.** Note that the **n-**at the

beginning of each use of **-ija** or the verb "to come" (see below) gives the sentence its Present Tense. This then means that, in Lukiga, we use "I am coming to . . ." or "We are coming to . . ." to infer what is going to be done in the future in much the same way the British say "I am going to . . ." or "We are going to . . .". It should be noted, however, that other forms of the Future Tense exist. For simplicity, I have referred to them minimally in the footnote[17] below.
The Future tense is constructed as follows:

Pronoun + **Ni-**future modifier + Root of the Verb "To Come" + Infinitive Form of the verb describing the expected action in future:

- **Nyowe ni + ny + ija kugyeenda. ¬ Nyowe ninyija kugyeenda.**
- Me, I will go. (Literally, "Me, I am coming to go.")

- **Iwe n + o + ija kugyeenda. ¬ Iwe noija kugyeenda.**
- (Singular) You, you will go. (Literally, "You, you are coming to go".)

- **We n + a + ija kugyeenda. ¬ We naija kugyeenda.**
- Him/Her, he/she will go. (Literally, "Him/Her, he/she is coming to go".)

- **Itwe ni + twi + ija kugyeenda. ¬ Itwe nitwiija kugyeenda.**
- We, we will go. (Literally, "We, are coming to go".)

- **Imwe ni + mwi + ija kugyeenda. ¬ Imwe nimwiija kugyeenda.**
- (Plural) You, you will go. (Literally, "You, you are coming to go".)

- **Bo ni + be + ija kugyeenda. ¬ Bo nibeija kugyeenda.**
- Them, they will go. (Literally, "Them, they are coming to go".)

Or, another form of the Future Tense is conjugated with what seems like a derivative of the verb "to eat", **okurya,** but is really just an

---
17

midfix that indicates future. This midfix is **-dya-** or **-rya-**. For example

- **Nyowe ndyagyeenda.**
  Informally, this often becomes **Ndyagyeenda.**
- Me, I will go. (Literally, "Me, I am coming to go".)

- **Iwe oryagyeenda.**
  Informally, this becomes **Oryagyeenda.**
- (Singular) You, you will go. (Literally, "You, you are coming to go".)

- **We aryagyeenda.**
  Informally, this becomes **Aryagyeenda.**
- Him/Her, he/she will go. (Literally, "Him/Her, he/she is coming to go".)

- **Itwe turyagyeenda.**
  Informally, this becomes **Turyagyeenda.**
- We, we will go. (Literally, "We, are coming to go".)

- **Imwe muryagyeenda.**
  Informally, this becomes **Muryagyeenda.**
- (Plural) You, you will go. (Literally, "You, you are coming to go".)

- **Bo baryagyeenda.**
  Informally, this becomes **Baryagyeenda.**
- Them, they will go. (Literally, "Them, they are coming to go".)

Yet another form of conjugation is common in Lukiga. This, for me, is incontrovertible evidence that some Bakiga had their ancestral origins in Rwanda or are closely related to or had an extensive period of contact with the Rwandans and their language before they travelled to Uganda.

- Instead of **Nyowe ninyija kugyeenda,** some Bakiga say, **Nyowe ndeija kugyeenda.**
- Me, I will go. (Literally, "Me, I am coming to go".)

- Instead of **Iwe noija kugyeenda,** some Bakiga say, **Iwe oreija kugyeenda.**

- Instead of **We neija kugyeenda,** some Bakiga say, **We areija kugyeenda.**

- Instead of **Itwe nitwiija kugyeenda,** some Bakiga say, **Itwe tureija kugyeenda.**

- Instead of **Imwe nimwiija kugyeenda,** some Bakiga say, **Imwe mureija kugyeenda.**

- Instead of **Bo nibeija kugyeenda,** some Bakiga say, **Bobareija kugyeenda.**

- (Singular) You, you will go. (Literally, "You, you are coming to go".)

- Him/Her, he/she will go. (Literally, "Him/Her, he/she is coming to go".)

- We, we will go. (Literally, "We, are coming to go".)

- (Plural) You, you will go. (Literally, "You, you are coming to go".)

- Them, they will go. (Literally, "Them, they are coming to go".)

Chapter Twenty-Two

THE SIMPLE PRESENT
EBIRIKUKORWA

Present in the following sentences takes the form of **n-** or **ni-**. This simple prefix creates the Simple Present Tense.

- I speak Lukiga.
- **Nyowe ningaamba orukiga.**

- You (singular) speak Lukiga.
- **Iwe nogaamba orukiga.**

- We speak Lukiga.
- **Itwe nitugaamba orukiga.**

- You (plural) speak Lukiga.
- **Imwe nimugaamba orukiga.**

- They speak Lukiga.
- **Bo nibagaamba orukiga.**

- It speaks Lukiga.
- **Yo negaamba orukiga.**

Note that the following midfixes represent the corresponding English personal pronouns and not the tense.

- I speak Lukiga.
- **Nyowe ningaamba orukiga.**

- You (singular) speak Lukiga.
- He/she speaks Lukiga.
- We speak Lukiga.
- You (plural) speak Lukiga.
- They speak Lukiga.
- It speaks Lukiga.

- **Iwe nogaamba orukiga.**
- **We nagaamba orukiga.**
- **Itwe nitugaamba orukiga.**
- **Imwe nimugaamba orukiga.**
- **Bo nibagaamba orukiga.**
- **Yo negaamba orukiga.**

Chapter Twenty-Three

THE PRESENT CONTINUOUS TENSE
EBIKWEISE NIBIKORWA

The Present Tense is conjugated with the verb "to hold", or **okukwaasa,** in its Present Tense form even though it is often dropped in the contracted form of use.

EXAMPLE

- **Nyowe nkweise ningyeenda.**
- Literally, "*Me, I am going*".

- **Nyowe**
- ¬ I (1st person singular), **n-**¬ (a prefix standing for and corresponding to the pronoun **Nyowe)-kweise** ¬ from the verb "to hold", which stands for an action taking place now in much the same way as the verb "to have" does in English.

- **ni-**
- Generally, **ni** by itself means "is" (the verb "to be"). This prefix signals that the Present Tense is in use here. This means that we should expect to find it wherever the Present Tense is used, and we do!

- **Nyowe n-kweise ni-n-gyeenda.**
- (I, I am going.) Here, I have italicised **ni-** to indicate that it is the marker of the Present Tense in this sentence.

- **We akweise na agyeenda.**
- This contracts to ¬ **We akweise nagyeenda.**

However, just to make life complicated, we have an alternative conjugation for the above example! As I have explained before, Lukiga, in particular, has two versions of the same conjugation.

- **Nyowe nkweise nda-gyeenda.**
- As I have suggested before, **da-** seems to have replaced the **ri-** that occurs in all the other conjugations for the Second Person Singular, Second Person Plural, Third Person Singular, Third Person Plural, and First Person Plural. See below.

- **Nyowe n-kweise n-da-gyeenda.**
- (I, I am going.) Here, again, **n-** is italicised to indicate that it is the marker of the Present Tense in this sentence.

- **We akweise ar-agyeenda.**
- This contracts to ¬ **We akweise nagyeenda.**

Apply the same analysis to the following sentences.

- **Iwe okweise (n)ogyeenda.**
  Alternative: **Iwe okweise oragyeenda.** Contracts to ¬ **Iw'okweis'oragyeenda.**

- (2ⁿᵈ Person Singular) ¬ You, you are going.

- **We akweise (n)agyeenda.**
  Alternative: **We akweise aragyeenda.** Contracts to ¬ **W'akweis'aragyeenda.**

- (3ʳᵈ Person Singular) ¬ Him/Her, he/she is going.

- **Itwe tukweise (ni) tugyeenda.**
  Alternative: **Itwe tukweise turagyeenda.** No contraction here because there are no vowels linking the words together.

- (1ˢᵗ Person Plural) ¬ We, we are going.

- **Imwe mukweise (ni) mugyeenda.**
  Alternative: **Imwe mukweise muragyeenda.** No contraction here because there are no vowels linking the words together.

- (2ⁿᵈ Person Plural) ¬ You, you are going.

- **Bo bakweise (ni) bagyeenda.**
  Alternative: **Bo bakweise baragyeenda.** No contraction here because there are no vowels linking the words together.

- (3ʳᵈ Person Plural) ¬ Them, they are going.

- **Yo ekweise (ni)egyeenda.**
  [*Becomes* ¬ **Yo ekweise negyeenda**]
  Alternative: **Yo ekweise eragyeenda.** Vowels are involved in linkage of words so we have contraction. ¬ **Yo ekweis' eragyeenda.**

- (3rd Person Singular) ¬ It, it is going.

In the following English examples, verbs and adverbs are treated equally ¬

- We are *going*.
- We are *well*.

In Lunyankole-Lukiga, however, there is a different indicator for the present where an adverb is concerned. (Remember, though, that rules are there to break!)

- We are going. ¬ **Itwe (tu)kweise (ni)(tu)gyeenda.**
- We are well. ¬ **Itwe tu-ri gye. (Gye** means well.)

The suffix **-ri** stands for something that is currently taking place. As explained in Chpater 24, it comes from the verb **okuba,** "to be". Thus, it serves as the present wherever an adverb, such as **gye,** occurs.

Review

- **Nyowe ndi kubi.** Or, **Nyowe ndi mubi.**
- I am bad.

- **Iwe ori kubi.** Or, **Iwe o-ri mubi.**
- You are bad.

- **We a-ri kubi.** Or, **We ni mubi.**
- He/She is bad.

- **Itwe turi kubi.** Or, **Itwe turi babi.**
- We are bad.

- **Imwe muri kubi.** Or, **Imwe muri babi.**
- You are bad.

- **Bo bari kubi.** Or, **Bo ni babi.**
- They are bad.

- **Yo eri kubi.** Or, **Yo ni mbi.**
- It is bad.

The following exercises will help to make the Present Tense familiar. Sometimes "now" or **hati** is used to help to emphasise the Present Tense:

- **Iwe nogyenda hati?**
- You, will you go now?

- **Imwe nimuteeka amate hati?**
- You, you boil the milk now?

- **Eego, itwe nituteeka amate hati.**
- Yes, we are boiling the milk now.

- **Bo nibagaruka ryari?**
- They, when are they coming back?

- **Bo nibagaruka nyenṣakare.**
- They, they will come back tomorrow.

- **Eṣther nateera omupiira ryari?**
- When will Esther play the ball?

- **Eṣther nateera omupiira aharwakataano.**
- Esther will play the ball on Friday.

- **Iwe wamuramuṣya ryari?**
- You, when did you greet him/her?

- **Nyowe namuramusya hati-hati!**
- **Abazeire bangye nibankuunda?**
- **Abazeire bangye nibankuunda.**

- I, I have greeted him just now!
- My parents, do they love me?
- My parents, they love me.

We never say,

- **Nyowe n-ri mubi.**
- **We a-ri mubi.** Or,
- **Bo bari babi.** Or,
- **Yo eri mbi**

Instead, we use odd forms to say,

- **Nyowe ndi mubi.**
- **We ni mubi.**
- **Bo ni babi.**
- **Yo ni mbi.**

So, we have,

- **Nyowe ndi mubi.**
- **Iwe ori mubi.**
- **We ni mubi.**
- **Itwe turi babi.**
- **Imwe muri babi.**
- **Bo ni babi.**
- **Yo ni mbi.**

Clearly, in some cases, the verb "to be" is preferred in the form **ni** and in the form **-ri** in others.

Chapter Twenty-Four

THE PAST PARTICIPLE
EBYAMARWA

PHOTO BY EDWARD NOBEL BISAMUNYU

KIGEZI HIGH SCHOOL STUDENTS HAVE COMPLETED A SUNDAY CHURCH SERVICE AT RUGARAMA HILL

ABAANA BA KIGEZI HIGH SCHOOL BAHEZA KUSHOMA OMUKANISA AHARI RUGARAMA

The Past Participle applies the verb "to be", **okuba.** The verb describing the action is also transformed largely by changing the ending to **-ire.** Very short contractions are possible in this and other tenses because midfix-prefixes still carry the meaning of the pronouns with which they correspond. Note that the midfix-prefixes accompanying the pronouns have changed slightly. Don't let them alarm you. They are the same as before but have only changed to ease speech. **Iwe o+aa-,** for example, produces **Iwe wa-.** This is probably the most difficult complex but once one understands how the **wa-**is arrived at then the path to it makes logical sense. Again, other forms of the Past Participle exist. See footnote[18] below.

- **Nyowe (n)-aaba nari-ire.**
- Me, I have eaten already. (Contraction ¬ **Nariire.**)

- **Iwe (w)-aaba wari-ire.**
- (Singular) You, you have eaten already. (Contraction ¬ **Wariire.**)

- **We (y)-aaba yari-ire.**
- Him/Her, he/she has eaten already.

- **Itwe (tw)-aaba twari-ire.**
- We, we have eaten already.

- **Imwe (mw)-aaba mwari-ire.**
- (Plural) You have eaten already.

---

[18] Using the verb "to leave", **okuruga,** we can conjugate as follows, leaving the verb of the action in its infinitive form ¬

1. **Nyowe naruga kurya.**
2. **Iwe waruga kurya.**
3. **We yaruga kurya.**
4. **Itwe twaruga kurya.**
5. **Imwe mwaruga kurya.**
6. **Bo baruga kurya.**

However, another form of conjugation uses the verb "to finish", **okuheza.** For example, we can write or say, **Nyowe naheza kurya,** which means, I have finished eating.

- **Bo (b)-aaba bari-ire.**
- Them, they have eaten already.

- **Yo (y)-aaba yariire.**
- It, it has eaten.

As in everything else in Lunyankole-Lukiga we can have contractions so that the table above is slightly transformed-by removing the box below-but renders the same meaning:

- **Nyowe (n)-aaba nari-ire.**
  This becomes ¬ **Nyowe naanariire.**
- Me, I have eaten already. (Contraction ¬ **Nariire.**)

- **Iwe (w)-aaba wari-ire.**
  This becomes ¬ **Iwe waawariire.**
- (Singular) You, you have eaten already. (Contraction ¬ **Wariire.**)

- **We (y)-aaba yari-ire.**
  This becomes ¬ **We yaayariire.**
- Him/Her, he/she has eaten already.

- **Itwe (tw)-aaba twari-ire.**
  This becomes ¬ **Itwe twaatwariire.**
- We, we have eaten already.

- **Imwe (mw)-aaba mwari-ire.**
  This becomes ¬ **Imwe mwaamwariire.**
- (Plural) You have eaten already.

- **Bo (b)-aaba bari-ire.**
  This becomes ¬ **Bo baabariire.**
- Them, they have eaten already.

- **Yo (y)-aaba yariire.**
  This becomes ¬ **Yo yaayariire.**
- It, it has eaten.

Chapter Twenty-Five

The Past Tense
Ebyamazirwe

We can achieve the Past Tense by inserting the midfix **-ka-** between the pronoun prefix and the verb.

- **Nyowe (n)-ka-gyeenda.**
- (1ˢᵗ Person Singular) ¬ Me, I went.

- **Iwe (o)-ka-gyeenda.**
- (2ⁿᵈ Person Singular) ¬ You, you went.

- **We (a)-ka-gyeenda.**
- (3ʳᵈ Person Singular) ¬ Him/Her, he/she is going.

- **Itwe (tu)-ka-gyeenda.**
- (1ˢᵗ Person Plural) ¬ We, we are going.

- **Imwe (mu)-ka-gyeenda.**
- (2ⁿᵈ Person Plural) ¬ You, you are going.

- **Bo (ba)-ka-gyeenda.**
- (3ʳᵈ Person Plural) ¬ Them, they are going.

- **Yo (e)kweise (ni)(e) gyeenda.**
- (3rd Person Singular) ¬ [*Becomes* ¬ **Yo ekweise negyeenda.**] It, it is going.

Other past tenses

A-ka-ba aba-ga murungyi. ¬ She used to be beautiful.

- **A**
  - He/She
- **-ka-**
  - midfix for past tense
- **-ba**
  - comes from the verb "to be", **okuba**
- **a-ba-**
  - Pronoun + root of the verb **okuba** but in connection with the suffix **-ga** gives us the "always" state in the sentence. This means that **Tu-ba-ga** indicates "we always are" and **Ba-ba-ga** stands for "they always are".
- **Akaba ari murungyi.**
  - She used to be beautiful.

In this sentence instead of **"abaga"** we have **"ari"**. The **-ba** stands for the verb **okuba,** to be. These are just very simple substitutions. **In ari,** the suffix **-ri** stands for the present so that **ari** means "he is" or "she is". However, it carries exactly the same meaning as **-ga** in the previous form.

Chapter Twenty-Six

Prepositions

Emyaanya

Prepositions, of course, are determinants of place or position or time in speech. Without them no language is able to describe precisely the relative positons of people and things. While these may be few in Lunyankole-Lukiga, they are still very important.

Lukiga	English
Aha	At
ahansi ya	"at the underside of"
Ahabwa	for ¬ literally, "at for"
ahaiguru ya	"on top of" or "above"
haihi na	near, next to
Na	with, and
Omu	In
Owa	To

Chapter Twenty-Seven

THE IMPERATIVE VERB
ENDAGYIRIRO

Imperative verbs, as in English, are infinitive verbs with the "to" removed! "To think" becomes "Think!" In Lunyankole-Lukiga, for example, "To think" is **o-ku-teekateeka.** Thus, our derived imperative verb, just as in English, is **Teekateeka!**

LUKIGA (SINGULAR)	LUKIGA (PLURAL)	ENGLISH
Garuka!	**Mugaruke!**	Come back!
Garula! Or **Garuza!**	**Mugarule!**	Bring back!
Gyeenda!	**Mugyeende!**	Go!
Handiika!	**Muhandiike!**	Write down!
Hangaara!	**Muhangaare!**	Long live!
Hanika!	**Muhanike!**	Hang! Or Hang up!
Hinga!	**Muhinge!**	Dig!

- **Ramusya!**
- **Muramusye!**
- Greet!

- **Rugaho!**
- **Murugeho!**
- Go away!

- **Shazamu!**
- **Mushazemu!**
- Cancel!

- **Shoborora!**
- **Mushoborore!**
- Explain!

- **Taaha!**
- **Mutaahe!**
- Go home!

- **Tangaara!**
- **Mutangaare!**
- Be filled with wonder!

- **Tangaaza!**
- **Mutangaaze!**
- Announce! Literally, "make wonderful!"

- **Tereera!**
- **Mutereere!**
- Straighten yourself!

- **Tereeza!**
- **Mutereeze!**
- Straighten something!

Negative Imperatives

In Lukiga, negative imperatives are obtained by inserting a **-ta-**midfix in the positive imperative. However, to this must also be added the relevant personal pronoun. Just as we have done in the middle column above, we can add various personal pronouns to the imperatives so that we are more person-specific in the instructions we give.

- **O-ta-garuka!**
- Don't (you, singular) come back!

- **Mu-ta-garuka!**
- Don't (you, plural) come back!

- **Mu-ta-garula!**
- Don't (you, plural) bring back!

- **Ba-ta-gyeenda!**
- Don't (they) go! *Or:* They don't go!

- **A-ta-handiika!**
- (He) don't write down! *Or:* He should not write down!

- **A-ta-ha-ngaara!**
- Don't live long!

- **Tu-ta-hanika!**
- We should not hang! *Or:* We should not hang up!

- **O-ta-hinga!**
- Don't (you) dig!

- **Ki-ta-ramusya!**
- It should not greet!

- **Ba-ta-rugaho!**
- They should not go away!

- **Zi-ta-shazamu!**
- They should not cancel! The **Zi-**here is a plural prefix for "it" in the **E-/Zi-**Noun Group.

- **Ba-ta-shoborora!**
- They should not explain!

- **Tu-ta-Taaha!**
- We should not go home!

- **Mu-ta-tangaara!**
- You must not be filled with wonder!

- **A-ta-tangaaza!**
- Announce! Literally, "make wonderful!"

- **O-ta-tereera!**
- Don't straighten yourself!

- **Tu-ta-tereeza!**
- We should not straighten (something)!

Chapter Twenty-Eight

Conditional Tenses
Kuri Nogyira

Photo by Edward Nobel Bisamunyu

Churchgoers at Rugarama Cathedral
Abashomi omu kanisa ya Rugarama

In this section it is important that you try and identify the function of each boxed item. Understanding its function will help you to see its usage and usefulness in Lunyankole-Lukiga. The small boxes bathed in grey indicate the critical prefix items that give sentences their conditional nature.

In the conditional tense, the word "if" is the critical marker or indicator of the condition. In Lunyankole-Lukiga, for "if" we use the prefix ku-. Various forms of its use are evident in Lukiga. As in English, "if" is a signal of regret or an expression of an inadequate circumstance. Again, as in English, "if" is sometimes equivalent to "when".

Given that **-ku-** is a common syllabic fixture in Lunyankole-Lukiga it is important that one is able to identify its usage as a marker of the condition. Clearly, as everything else in language, it would be very easy to fail to pick it up in a sentence if one has not practised its use or recognition.

Present Conditional Tense

Nyowe ku n-di-kuza owa mukaaka ni-mu-twar-ira omugaati.

Or:

Ku n-za-ga owa mukaaka ni-mutwarira-ga omugaati.

Or:

Ku ndi-kuza owa mukaaka mu-twarira-ga omugaati. (This sentence is the same as the two above but drops the personal pronoun **ni-,** probably because it is used in the first part of the sentence already.)

Vocabulary and explanation:

okuza ¬ to go somewhere; also appears as **-za** in this sentence; owa ¬ possessive pronoun [of] for a noun in the **O-/A-**Group; **mukaaka** ¬ grandmother; **okutwarira** ¬ to take something to or for somebody; the **-ga** following **-za** and **nimutwarira-** indicates something that was done frequently or repeatedly or always but only in the past or recent past. Thus, it helps to emphasise the condition as having been permanent; **omugaati** ¬ bread

This tense (or sentence) talks about something that happens often. The first box **Ku** in the sentence is an expression of the condition. The second box **ndi** stands for the pronoun of the person or subject, which is, in this case, I.

Ku ari-kuza owa mukaaka a-mu-twarira omugaati.

Or:

Ku a-za-ga owa mukaaka a-mutwarira-ga omugaati.

Ku tu-ri-kutunga ekihumuuro nzaga kureeba Muhabuura.

Or:

Ku tu-tunga ekihumuuro nzaga kureeba Muhabuura.

Ku ba-ri-kutunga ekihumuro bazaga kureeba Muhabuura.

Or:

Ku-ba-tunga ekihumuro bazaga kureeba Muhabuura.

Vocabulary and explanation:

Same as above except for the subject, which, in this case, is he/she, as indicated by the pronoun **-ari-**.

In the second sentence here we have **a** without the **-ri-,** which is in this case treated as unnecessary because the **-ga** serves the same purpose of indicating time or frequency.

Vocabulary and explanation:

okutunga ¬ to obtain; **ekihumuuro** ¬ a holiday; **okureeba** ¬ to see or to visit; **tu** ¬ the pronoun we; **Muhabuura** ¬ the prominent mountain in SW Uganda

In the second sentence here **tu** is without the **-ri-**for the same reasons we have indicated above. Note n as the pronoun I.

Vocabulary and explanation:

We have only one change here: the personal pronoun **-ba-,** which indicates "they".

Past Conditional Tense

- **Ira**

This three-letter word is an important reference to history or ancient times. I have no firm evidence that this is true but the suffix **-ire,** which often helps to indicate an action that took place some time ago, may be related to or have its origin in this word. For example, **obeire** means "a person who was".

Ku wa-beire o-tayaaya okaba o-gyenda nobushera.

Vocabulary:

Wabeire: wa ¬ pronoun prefix for "you"
-beire ¬ comes from the verb "to be",
okuba but refers to the past tense; **o-**¬ pronoun prefix that accompanies **wa-**
okutayaaya ¬ to visit
okaba ¬ from the verb "to be"; used to be
obushera ¬ a sweet but non-alcoholic sorghum drink brewed by every self-respecting home in Kigezi

Ku wa-ba-ga o-tayaay-ire o-kaba o-gyendana-ga n'obushera.

Vocabulary and explanation:

okugyenda ¬ to go
okaba ¬ literally, "you used to be"

Ku-twa-be-ire tu-tayaaya tukaba tugyendana-ga nobuṣhera.

Or:

Ku-twa-be-ire tutayaayaga tukabatugyendana-ga nobuṣhera.

Vocabulary and explanation:

Use the knowledge you have acquired so far from the preceding explanations to understand this.

Ku wa-tayaay-ire okagyenda nobuṣhera.

Vocabulary and explanation:

This sentence is different in the sense that it describes what happened on only one occasion rather than what usually happened in the past. In other words, even though it comes under a similar tense it is about an event that was not habitual.

FUTURE CONDITIONAL TENSE

There must be, of course, some marker or indication of the future in this tense. Instead of the word "will" Lunyankole-Lukiga employs the verb "to come" to indicate that the action described by the primary verb will take place in future.

In the general future tense, we use the midfix **-rya-** to indicate something that shall be done. So, for example, we can say, **A-rya-za London,** or, "He/She will go to London". In the Future Conditional Tense, however, we apply **-ri-**. For example, **Ku a-ri-za London . . ."**

Ku n-di-za Kabale ninyija kuroonda munywaani wangye.

Vocabulary and explanation:

okwiija ¬ to come ¬ we use this verb in Lunyankole-Lukiga to indicate that an action will take place in future.

okuroonda ¬ to look for

ni-ny- ¬ personal pronoun + connector to the verb root **-ija-**(to come)

The verb **okuza** gives us useful modifiers to help show that a sentence is talking about an action in the future.

The suffix modifiers **-za** and **-aze** are both derived from this verb.

Ku nda-a-ze Kabale ni-ny-ija kuroonda munywaani wangye.

Vocabulary and explanation:
omunywaani ¬ a friend
Otherwise, apply information given in previous explanation.

Ku nda-a-ze owa mukaaka ndyamutwarira omugaati.

Vocabulary and explanation:

[Note how different this sentence is from a similar sentence in the Present Conditional Tense above. So, even though they are both conditional one expresses something that may always happen and the other something that may happen once in the future.]

Ku-tu-ri-garuka omuka ni-twi-ija kushemererwa.	Vocabulary and explanation: "When we shall return home we will be happy".
Ku-abaana ba-ri-garuka omuka abazeire baabo nibeija kushemerererwa.	Vocabulary and explanation: "When the children shall return their parents will be happy".

Or:

Ku-abaana ba-ri-garuka omuka abazeire baabo baryashemerererwa.	"When the children shall return their parents will be happy".

THE CONTINUOUS CONDITIONAL TENSE

A song we learned in the Christian church service's Sunday School in Kabale and indeed other childhood wishes made the clear purpose and point of creating the conditional tense.

Kuri nyine amapapa	If I had wings,
Nkabeire malaika,	I would be an angel,
Nkagurukire mpikayo	And fly my way and reach -
Omunsi Sayuuni!	The land of Zion!

We also have in Lunyankole-Lukiga a proverb, **Kuri namanyire eyija bwanyima!** This means, "If I had known comes afterwards!"

Kuri nogyira ngu omushana nigujwa tukayerize omugusha!	Literally, "If you were to imagine the sun shining we would achieve a harvest of sorghum".
Kuri nogyira ngu omushana nigujwa bakayerize omugusha!	Literally, "If you were to imagine the sun shining they would achieve a harvest of sorgum.

Kuri nimanya ngu nankuunda tinkabuzire busingye.

Literally, "If I knew that he/she loved me I would not be so unhappy".

Kuri namanyire ngu nankuunda tinkagayeire.

Literally, "If I had known that he/she loved me I would not be so unhappy".

Chapter Twenty-Nine

Possessive Pronouns
Bituungw'oha?

Photo by Edward Nobel Bisamunyu

A Young Band Hopeful
Omwaana orikweshuunga banda munonga!

Unlike English Lukiga and Lunyankole do not have possessive pronouns. Instead, they have possessive suffixes, which are placed after the word of. So, for example, rather than speak of "my ball" a Mukiga would say "ball of mine".

The "of" in Lunyankole-Lukiga and other Bantu languages is not the one-size-fits-all that is used in English: *a man of power, a girl of mine, a vicar of the village church, etc.* In Lukiga, of is tailored to suit the noun through its specific group. Since we are now quite familiar with nouns in the People Group **(Omu-/Aba-),** let us use examples from there to illustrate how possessives are used in Lunyankole-Lukiga.

There are two possessive suffixes for each noun group, one for the singular and one for the plural. If I am speaking about "my teacher" in the People Group, I have to say **"Omushomesa wangye"** for the singular and **"Abashomesa bangye"** for the plural. We know, already, that most nouns describing people begin with **omu-** for singular and **aba-** for plural. The suffix that represents "my" in Lukiga is **-angye.** Before this suffix, we must have **wa-** or **ba-,** which represent "of" for singular and plural forms respectively.

Possessive Adjective in Singular Form	Possessive Adjective in Plural Form
• **Omushomesa wa-angye**	• My teacher
• **Abashomesa ba-angye**	• My teachers
• **Omwegyesa waangye**	• My teacher
• **Abegyesa baangye**	• My teachers
• **Omwami waangye**	• My boss
• **Abaami baangye**	• My bosses or my chiefs
• **Omwami waangye**	• My husband
• **Abaami baangye**	• My husbands
• **Omukazi**[19] **waangye**	• My wife
• **Abakazi baangye**	• My wives
• **Omurweire waangye**	• My patient
• **Abarweire baangye**	• My patients

---

[19] Omukazi is very informal indeed! Literally, it means "my woman". A more formal term would be "Omukyara wangye", which translates as "my lady".

- **Omwaana waangye** — My baby or my child
- **Abaana baangye** — My babies or my children
- **Omupakazi waangye** — My labourer
- **Abapakazi baangye** — My labourers
- **Omuṣhaija waangye** — My man
- **Abaṣhaija baangye** — My men
- **Omwoojo waangye** — My boy
- **Aboojo baangye** — My boys
- **Omwiṣhiki waangye** — My daughter or my girl
- **Abaiṣhiki baangye** — My daughters or my girls
- **Omuhara waangye** — My daughter or my girl
- **Abahara baangye** — My daughters or my girls
- **Omutṣigazi waangye** — My son or my young man
- **Abatṣigazi baangye** — My sons or my young men
- **Omutabani waangye** — My son
- **Abatabani baangye** — My sons
- **Omurumuna waangye** — My sibling (if of the same sex)
- **Abarumuna baangye** — My siblings (if of the same sex)
- **Muzaara**[20] **waangye** — My cousin
- **Bazaara baangye** — My cousins

Some person-nouns can be confusing! "Sister", for example, is **munyanya** and "sisters" are **banyanya.** The respective **o-**and **a-**prefixes are always missing. In other words, it is never **o-munyanya** or **a-banyanya!**

---

[20] *Omuzaara or muzaara seems to have the same root as the verb okuzaara. This indicates that the relationship may be named after the fact of being born together, as cousins surely are! In English this literally refers to births that are contemporaneous or contemporary. In Lukiga, inferred in this meaning is the supportive role played by cousins even in the process of being born. It is, however, not always thus! Cousins, naturally, may be arch-antagonists of each other.*

Some person-nouns, like **munyanya,**[21] instead of applying the possessive suffix **-angye,** use the suffix **-zi** at their end. For example, we can say,

- **Munyanya-zi/banyanya-zi** ¬ My sister/my sisters

The **-zi** suffix may come from the word **omuzi/emizi** ¬ root/roots. Hence, "my sister" may mean "root-sister", or "sister from the same roots". This is sheer supposition on my part but it makes perfect sense given that Lukiga and Lunyankole languages have vocabulary that may seem to be far-fetched in other languages. So, whether my analysis here is weak or not is not the question but it is certainly a suggestion that begs academic research.

Now, we can add the other possessive suffixes! Each pronoun has its own possessive suffix. We have just dealt with "mine" for the First Person Singular. However, let's first learn the word equivalent for "and" in Lukiga and Lunyankole. It is **na.** So, if we are discussing two people as the subject of a sentence we speak of them as "**Edward na Edmund**" or Edward and Edmund.

- **A na B**
- **Anna na Benita**
- **X na Y**
- **Uganda na Kenya**
- **Posh na David**

The Second Person Singular, "You", is **Iwe** in Lukiga and Lunyankole. If we are talking about "you and your cousin" we would say **"iwe na muzaara w-aawe".** The possessive suffix for "your" or "yours" is **-awe.** Hence, we can say,

- **Iwe na muzaara waawe.**
- **Iwe na mutabani waawe.**
- **Iwe n'omukyaara waawe.**

---

[21] Not to be confused with *Enyanya*. This means tomato in both singular and plural forms!

For the Third Person Singular, the possessive suffix for 'his' or 'her' is -eye.

- **We na muzaara w-eye.** This is the same as: **We na muzaara we.**
- **We na mutabani w-eye.** This is the same as: **We na mutabani we.**
- **We n'omukyaara w-eye.** This is the same as: **We n'omukyaara we.**

For the First Person Plural, the possessive suffix for 'ours' is -eitu.

- **Itwe na bazaara b-eitu.**
- **Itwe na batabani b-eitu.**
- **Itwe n'abakyaara b-eitu.**

For the Second Person Plural, the possessive suffix for 'your' or 'yours' is -anyu.

- **Imwe na muzaara w-anyu.**
- **Imwe na bazaara b-anyu.**
- **Imwe na batabani b-anyu.**

For Third Person Plural, the possessive suffix for "theirs" is -aabo.

- **Bo na bazaara b-aabo.**
- **Bo na batabani b-aabo.**
- **Bo n'abakyaara b-aabo.**

Chapter Thirty

Relative Pronouns
Enyorekyerero

Photo by Edward Nobel Bisamunyu

Buses in Hong Kong
Baasi omuri Hong Kong

In Lukiga and Lunyankole the relevant group prefixes serve as relative pronouns. For example, when we are talking about a person, **omuntu,** we use the prefix relative to the singular of the Human Noun Group, **omu-.** Similarly, for the plural, **abantu,** we apply the prefix **aba-.** The verb okukiza means to cure or to bring about healing. It comes from the verb to heal, or, **okukira.**

English equivalent	Full translation	Contracted translation with the subject pronoun removed
The spy who loved me!	**Omubegi owa-nkunzire!**	**Owankunzire!**
The spies who loved me!	**Ababegi aba-nkunzire!**	**Abankunzire!**
The doctor who cured me.	**Omushaho owa-n-ki-ri-ze.**	**Owankirize.**
The doctor who has cured me.	**Omushaho o-wa-n-ki-z-a.** (Past Participle)	**Owankiza.**
The doctors who cured me.	**Abashaho abankirize.**	**Abankirize.**

For nouns in the **O-A** Noun Group, the relative prefix for singular is **oku-**, and the prefix for plural is **aga-**.

- **Okuguru oku-ri-kushaasha.** ¬ The leg which is hurting. (The -ri-midfix here puts the sentence in the present.)
- **Amaguru aga-ri-ushaasha.** ¬ The legs which are hurting.

- **Okutu oku-na-hurizize.** ¬ The ear with which I heard.
- **Amatu agu-na-huriize.**

For nouns in the **E-A** Noun Group, the relative prefix for singular is **eri-**, and the prefix for plural is **agu-**.

- **Eriisho eri-na-huteiz-e.** ¬ The eye that I injured. (Or: The Eye that got injured.)

- **Eirebe eri-ndi-ku-kuund-a.** ¬ The water lily that I like. This is in the present continuous tense, hence the use of the infinitive verb root.

Chapter Thirty-One

Our Adjectives
Enshoboorozi

Photo by Edward Nobel Bisamunyu

Supersized buildings on the north side of Zhengzhou, Henan, China
Ebyombeko bya kagaanga (nainga rutaaba) omuri Zhengzhou, Henan, China!

An adjective, in Lukiga, occupies a position after the noun. So, we have something like "a book black" or "the man tall". This is a very easy adjustment to make for an English-speaking person. However, the challenge lies in learning to use a specific adjectival prefix for each noun depending on the noun group in which it is found.

In applying adjectives we have to look at the noun in question and apply its relative prefix to the adjective. In singular form a noun has one prefix and another in its plural form. For example ¬
Using Adjectives in the Human (**Omu-/Aba-**) Group

- **Omuntu mu-hango** ¬ A big person
- **Abantu ba-hango** ¬ Big people
- **Omuntu mu-rungyi** ¬ A beautiful person
- **Abantu ba-rungyi** ¬ Beautiful people

Let us first look at some adjectives so that we have them to work with. We can see from the two examples I have given above that adjectives have root words to which we can attach group-determined prefixes. Let's learn some adjective roots¬

Note that adjectives that have the additional **-ri-** at their start are probably employing a remnant of the verb *to be*. In other words, if a kettle is black we say, "It is black" in a very awkward way that means, literally, "Which is black". This is stated as a complete sentence rather than the descriptive clause that it is in English. That means or infers, of course, *a black kettle*. In Lukiga, this would be, ***"Ebinika e-ri-kwiragura",*** or, *"The kettle that is black".* Other adjectives, however, as shown below, are adequate without the influence of the verb *to be*.

- **-aingyi**
- **-bi**
- **-bisi**
- **-gufu**
- **-gumire**
- **-haango**
- **-kazi**

- Many
- ugly, bad
- raw, unripe
- Short
- hard, difficult
- Big
- Female

- **-kuru**
- **-kuru**
- **-kye**
- **-kye**
- **-maanzi**
- **-orobi**
- **-reingwa**
- **-ri-kutukura**
- **-ri-kwiragura**
- **-ri-nganiire**
- **-rungyi**
- **-shariira**
- **-to**
- **-nuzire**
- **-gubire**
- **-omire**

- old, great
- old, senior, respected, adult
- small, little
- Few
- courageous, brave
- soft, easy
- tall, long
- Red
- Black
- moderate, medium
- beautiful, good, nice
- bitter, sour
- young, new
- sweet, tasty
- Dirty
- Dry

Adjectives in the Ki-Bi Group

Clearly, to use adjectives one must be aware of which noun group they have come from. If we wanted to apply an adjective to describe a book, its subject prefix would have to preced the adjective. As the noun book, **ekitabo,** belongs to the **Eki-Bi** Noun Group, the adjective would have to be preceded by the relevant ki-prefix. If, however, the plural were involved, the prefix would have to be **bi-.**

- **Ekitabo ki-haango** ¬ a large book
- **Ebitabo bi-haango** ¬ large books

- **Ekitabo ki-rungyi** ¬ a good book/a beautiful book
- **Ebitabo bi-rungyi** ¬ beautiful books

- **Ekimera ki-gufu** ¬ a short plant
- **Ebimera bi-gufu** ¬ short plants

We can now apply prefixes to the adjectives given above, using the appropriate prefixes. For the first part write the English equivalent of each sentence.

- **Ekiteengye ki-gufu**
- **Ebiteengye bi-gufu**
- **Ekigyere ki-kuru**
- **Ebigyere bi-kuru**
- **Ekitanda ki-reingwa**
- **Ebitanda bi-reingwa**
- **Ekyanzi ki-rungyi**
- **Ebyanzi bi-rungyi**
- **Ekinoombe ki-gumire**
- **Ebinoombe bi-gumire**

ADJECTIVES IN THE **E-AMA** GROUP

In this group the singular (**E-**) takes the prefix **ri-**, and the plural (**Ama-**) takes the prefix **ma-**.

- **Eihuri ri-haango. Amahuri ma-haango**
- **Eishomero ri-rungyi. Amashomero ma-rungyi**
- **Eirwariro ri-bi. Amarwariro ma-bi**
- **Eichumu ri-reingwa. Amacumu ma-reingwa**

There is, however, in the plural, use of a different prefix, **ga-**, when the adjective ends in **-ire** or **-ira**.

- **Eihega ri-gumire**
- **Amahega ga-gumire**
- **Eryanda ri-rikwiragura**
- **Amanda ga-rikwiragura**
- **Eishaza** (sometimes called **eisaza**) **ri-rikutukura**
- **Amashaza** (or **amasaza**) **ga-rikutukura**
- **Eitembero ri-gumire**
- **Amatembero ga-gumire**

ADJECTIVES IN THE **OMU-EMI** GROUP

In this group the singular (O) takes the prefix **gu-** and plural (E) takes the prefix **e-**.

Omugongo gu-rweire
Emigongo e-rweire

- **Omugongo/emigongo** ¬ A back/backs
- **Omukono/emikono** ¬ An arm/arms
- **Omushozi/emishozi** ¬ A hill/hills
- **Omuze/emize** ¬ A habit/habits
- **Omurabyo/emirabyo** ¬ A lightning/lightning(s)
- **Omuserebende/emiserebende** ¬ A limousine/limousines
- **Omurundi/emirundi** ¬ A time/times (Think of multiplication!)
- **Omurundi/emirundi** ¬ A tibia/tibias (Think of a leg bone!)
- **Omugaanda/emigaanda** ¬ A bundle/bundles
- **Omuguha/emiguha** ¬ A rope/ropes
- **Omweenda/emyeenda** ¬ A piece of cloth or clothing/pieces of cloth or clothing
- **Omuhoro/emihoro** ¬ A sickle/sickles
- **Omupiira/emipiira** ¬ A ball/balls
- **Omuriro/emiriro** ¬ A fire/fires
- **Omuze/emize** ¬ A habit/habits
- **Omuzi/emizi** ¬ A root/roots
- **Omuti/emiti** ¬ A tree/trees
- **Omutumba[22]/emitumba** ¬ A banana tree/banana trees

The Oku-/Ama-Noun Group

- **Okuguru/amaguru** ¬ A leg/legs
- **Okuju/amaju** ¬ A knee/knees
- **Okwaahwa/amaahwa** ¬ An armpit/armpits
- **Okutu/amatu** ¬ An ear/ears
- **Obwaato/amaato** ¬ A boat or canoe or ship/Boats or canoes or ships

---

[22] Not to be confused with "Omutumbi" and "Emitumbi", which mean "corpse" and "corpses", respectively!

The E-/E-Group (Countables)

In both the singular and plural groups the names are exactly the same. Thus, we have **esigara emwe** (one cigarette) or **esigara ibiri** (two cigarettes).

- **Entabire** ¬ a garden row /rows in a garden[23]
- **Enda** ¬ a stomach; a pregnancy
- **Endeeba** ¬ a look/looks (the way somebody looks with their eyes: one can look to insult another, for example)
- **Enoono** ¬ a heel/heels
- **Enkuumba** ¬ a woman who cannot conceive
- **Enkuundwakazi** ¬ the favourite wife (in a polygamous household)
- **Engaro** ¬ a hand/hands
- **Ebisya** ¬ a neck/necks
- **Engabo** ¬ a shield/shields
- **Enyungu** ¬ a pot/pots

The Or-Group:
(Some Uncountables)

- **Orwaamba** ¬ Blood from livestock (for cooking)
- **Orwaari** ¬ Noise
- **Orwambiza** ¬ a mess, chaos

The Om-Group
(More Uncountables)

- **Omuraamba** ¬ beer

---

[23] In certain gardens, some food crops are sown or planted in raised rows to enable them to drain properly. Sweet potato gardens in Kigezi provide a good example.

Chapter Thirty-Two

OUR ADVERBS
EMITWARIZE

PHOTO BY EDWARD NOBEL BISAMUNYU

SUPERFAST JET PLANES AT NAIROBI AIRPORT, KENYA
ENDEGYE ZIRIKWIRUKA MUNONGA AHA KISHAAHA KY'ENDEGYE NAIROBI, KENYA

Adverbs in Lukiga are derived from adjectives. Generally, we obtain an adverb by taking the suffix of an adjective and giving it the prefix **oku-** or **ku-.** This prefix stands for "how" and infers the way in which something is done. For example, to say "I will treat her well" one writes **Ninyija kumutwaara ku-rungyi,** or, literally, "I will come to take her well". It is this **-rungyi** root that corresponds to "well" or "good" or "beautiful". Faithfulness to the standard, which does not shift, is implied here by the prefix **ku-.** For example, even when an action is in the past tense we still say, **Nkamutwaara ku-rungyi,** or, "I treated her well", literally, "I took her well" because this is something

166

that is universally understood to be good. Like the **ku-**in Lukiga, -ly stands for how something is done.

PHOTO BY EDWARD NOBEL BISAMUNYU

A VERY OLD CAR: **EMOTOKA NKURU MUNONGA**

EXAMPLES OF THE USE OF ADVERBS:

1. **Kandi nayeshongora kurungyi.** ¬ And she sings beautifully.
2. **Omukyaara Yohaana nayetwaara gye.** ¬ Mrs Yohaana conducts/carries herself well.
3. **"Mpora-mpora" ekahisya omunyongororwa ahaiziba.** [A Lukiga-Lunyankole proverb] ¬ The slow pace eventually brought a worm to the well. Literally: "Slowly-slowly" took a worm to the well. I have placed this in quotes because it is actually spoken of as a policy rather than a description of the worm's movement. Technically, then, this is not an adverb here but a commendable policy or philosophy!
4. **Gyenda mpora mwaana!** ¬ Go slowly, child! (This wisdom is imparted to many a Mukiga child during their upbringing.)
5. **Gyenda juba mwaana!** ¬ The opposite wisdom to that given above.

6. **Amagezi ga wakame nokungyenda *mpora.*** [Proverb] ¬ The cleverness of the hare/rabbit derives from moving carefully. [The Bakiga, at least in language, equate being careful with going slowly. The name Nyabwangu refers to a girl who works in a hurry, often bungling things!]

We have, in Lukiga, other adverbs which, in English, relate to how one wants something done. The prefix **oku-** literally stands for how. So, if we say

- **Okunayenzire** ¬ as I wanted, or, the way I wanted
- **Okuyanshabire** ¬ as he or she asked me (to do)
- **Okunabasiize** ¬ as I could
- **Okunabweine** ¬ as I found
- **Okutwayenzire** ¬ as we wished, as we wanted
- **Okubatushabire** ¬ as they asked us (to do)
- **Okutwabasiize** ¬ as we could
- **Okutwabweine** ¬ as we found

Conjunctions

But

- **Kwonka**[11] ¬ But

Example ¬ **Omwaana yaija *kwonka* nyina tinamureeba.**

¬ The child came but I did not see its mother.

Although

- **Nobu** ¬ Although

Example ¬ ***Nobu* araabe arweire neija kuza ahamizaano.**

¬ Although he is ill, he will attend the sports.

Because

- **Ahabwokuba** ¬ Because
Example ¬ **Ninyija kwija ahabwokuba John akanyeta.**

¬ I will come because John invited me.

But

- **Kwonka**[24] ¬ But
Example ¬ **Omwaana yaija kwonka nyina tinamureeba.**

¬ The child came but I did not see its mother.

But

- **Kwonka**[11] ¬ But
Example ¬ **Omwaana yaija kwonka nyina tinamureeba.**

¬ The child came but I did not see its mother.

Although

- **Nobu** ¬ Although
Example ¬ **Nobu araabe arweire neija kuza ahamizaano.**

¬ Although he is ill, he will attend the sports.

---

[24] Not to be confused with okwonka, to breast-feed!

Because

- **Ahabwokuba** ¬ Because
  Example ¬ **Ninyija kwija ahabwokuba John akanyeta.**

  ¬ I will come because John invited me.

So, given that, then

- **Mbwenu** ¬ So, then, given that
  Example ¬ **Mbwenu kunamurebire nairuka atyo natangaara.**

  ¬ So when I saw him running like that I was astonished.

As, when

- **Ku** ¬ As, when
  Example ¬
  Ku-na-mu-rebire nairuka atyo natangaara!

  ¬ When I saw him running like that I was astonished!

So, therefore

- **Nahabwekyo** ¬ Therefore
  (Literally means "because of that" or "for that reason".)
  Example ¬ **Nahabwekyo ninkushaba omuyaambe.**

  ¬ Therefore, I ask you to help him/her.

Except

- **Okwihaho** ¬ With the exception of ¬ **Okwihaho abaana bato, abandi mugyende!** — Except young children, others go!

INTERJECTIONS

- **Eego** or **Eeeh,** or **Yeee** ¬ Yes
- **Ngaaha** ¬ No
- **Mpora,** or **Huumura**[25] ¬ Sorry or Relax

DEMONSTRATIVE PRONOUNS

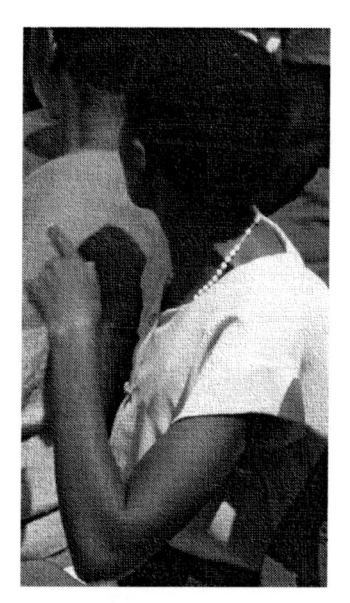

PHOTO BY EDWARD NOBEL BISAMUNYU

A MUKIGA WOMAN IN KABALE: THAT'S HIM!
OMUKAZI WOMUKIGA OMURI KABALE: NIWOOGWE!

---

[25] *Mpora* means 'Slow!' and *Huumura* means 'Rest!' or 'Relax!'

1. **-gyi** ¬ this
2. **-bi** ¬ these
3. **-gyo** or **-ri** or **-riiya** ¬ that
4. **-ebyo** ¬ those
5. **-gu** ¬ this (person)
6. **-gwe** ¬ that (person)
7. **-ba** ¬ these (people)
8. **-bo** ¬ those (people)

Usage in Lukiga

- **Abahara aba!**
- **Abahara abo!**
- **Abajungu abo!**
- **Abakiga abo!**
- **Abantu aba.**
- **Abantu abo!**
- **Abantu bariiya!**
- **Akantu ako!**
- **Akantu kariiya!**
- **Akashanduko ako!**
- **Akati aka!**
- **Akati ako!**
- **Ebintu ebi.**
- **Ebintu ebyo!**
- **Ebiti ebyo!**
- **Ekintu ekyi.**
- **Ekiti ekyo!**
- **Emiti eriya!**
- **Omuntu ogu.**
- **Omuti guri!**
- **Omuti ogu!**
- **Omuti ogwe!**
- **Oruntu oru!**
- **Abahara aba!**
- **Abahara abo!**
- **Abajungu abo!**
- **Abakiga abo!**

English Translation

- These girls!
- Those girls!
- Those Europeans!
- Those Bakiga!
- These people!
- Those people!
- Those people!
- That thing!
- That thing!
- That little suitcase!
- This little stick!
- That little stick!
- These things!
- Those things!
- Those sticks!
- This thing!
- That stick!
- Those trees!
- This person!
- That tree!
- This tree!
- That tree!
- This thing (very large)!
- These girls!
- Those girls!
- Those Europeans!
- Those Bakiga!

- **Abantu aba!**
- **Abantu abo!**

- These people!
- Those people!

Interrogative Pronouns

- **Niinye?**
- **Niiwe?**
- **Niwe?**
- **Nikyo? Niko? Nitwo? Nibwo?**
- **Nirwo?**
- **Niitwe?**
- **Niimwe?**
- **Nibo?**
- **Oha?** (Sometimes **Ni oha?** This often contracts to **Nooha?** > It is who?)
- **Baaha (Ni baaha?)**
- **Kiiha, kaaha, tuuha, ruuha, guuha, gaaha?**
- **Nkahe (Ni nkahe?)**
- **Ota?**
- **Ryaari?**
- **Ni-zi-ngahe?**

- **Ni-bi-ngahe?**

- Me?
- You?
- Him? Her?
- It? It? Them (diminutive), Them (diminutive)

- We?
- You? (Plural)
- Them?
- Who? Whom?

- Who? (Plural)
- Which?

- Where?
- How?
- When?
- How much is it? ¬ For a question about the quantity of a noun in the **E-E** Noun Group in plural form.
- How much is it? ¬ For a question about the quantity of a noun in the **KI-BI** Noun Group in plural form.

Chapter Thirty-Three

Our Relationships
Abanyabuzaare

Relationships have interesting names in Lunyankole-Lukiga. We, for example, are said to have fathers and younger fathers! The list below will, I think, speak for itself!

- **Taata** — Father
- **Maama neinga Maawe** — Mother
- **Shwento** — Paternal uncle (Literally, Younger Father)
- **Maawento neinga nyokwento** — Maternal aunt
- **Sho** — Your father
- **Nyoko** — Your mother
- **Omurumuna** — Brother
- **Munyanyazi** — My sister
- **Shwenkuru** — Grandfather
- **Maawenkuru neinga Nyokwenkuru neinga Mukaaka** — Grandmother
- **Shwenkazi** — Paternal aunt
- **Taatazaara** — Father-in-law
- **Maazaara** — Mother-in-law
- **Nyokorume** — Maternal uncle
- **Omutabani** — Son

- **Omuhara**
- **Omuramu**
- **Omuramukazi**
- **Omukwe**
- **Omwiihwa**
- **Omukamwaana**

- Girl, daughter
- An in-law
- A female in-law
- An in-law
- Your sister's child
- The wife of your son

Photo by Edward Nobel Bisamunyu

Kampala Taxi Park
Obuhumuriro bw'emotoka za taxi

Chapter Thirty-Four

SUBJECT & OBJECT PRONOUNS
AMAZIINA GA BYOONA

Subject and object pronouns in Lukiga are represented by prefixes and midfixes. We have already seen subject pronouns ¬

- **Nyowe** ¬ I
- **Iwe** ¬ You (singular)
- **We** or **Uwe** (read "way") ¬ He/She [Yes! We have one pronoun-word for male and female!]
- **Itwe** ¬ We
- **Imwe** ¬ You (plural)
- **Bo** (pronounced with or without aspiration depending on dialect) ¬ They

Object pronouns are similar but are represented by midfixes. The object midfix comes before the verb root, as shown in the given example below.

Object midfix
- **-n-**
- **-ku-**
- **-mu-**
- **-ba-**

What it stands for
- stands for "me"
- stands for "you"
- stands for "him/her"
- (pronounced with aspiration, so that it sounds like "bha-") means "them"

- **-tu-**
- **-ba-**

- stands for "us"
- * same as "them" (pronounced with aspiration "bha") means "you"

Let us explain this by example ¬

EXAMPLE 1

Preparatory vocabulary ¬

- **Okuyaamba** ¬ to help
- **Omushomesa/Abashomesa** ¬ A teacher/teachers

A teacher helped his student with his homework. Our sentence about it is simple¬ *He helped him.* In Lunyankole-Lukiga, it is just as simple, involving the insertion of an appropriate midfix!

- **Akamuyaamba.**

When we analyse this we see that it is made up of four parts. The first is the pronoun prefix **A-,** which stands for "He" or "She", the subject of this sentence; the second is the midfix **-ka-,** which indicates Past Tense; the third is the midfix **-mu-,** which represents the object of the sentence and refers to "him" or "her"; and the last part stands for the verb **okuyaamba,** or 'to help'.

A-ka-mu-yaamba.

- **A** ¬ Stands for **"He".** This is the subject pronoun.
- **-ka-**¬ Represents an action in the past tense
- **-mu-**¬ This is the object pronoun standing for the student.
- **-yaamba** ¬ This is the verb describing what the subject did.

Our sentence literally reads as follows ¬

[He/She] [in the past] [him/her] [help]. OR ¬ *He or she helped him.*

Example 2

Preparatory vocabulary ¬

- **oku-kunda** ¬ to love
- **omwaana/abaana** ¬ A child/children
- **nyina** ¬ mother
- **-we** ¬ its

The child loves its mother. ¬ **Omwaana na-kunda nyina-we.** Here, we can replace "its mother" **(nyinawe)** with the appropriate object pronoun "her", **-mu-**. Keep in mind that in Lunyankole-Lukiga, object pronouns are gender-neutral. However, as in English, they indicate that the object is a person or people, or a thing or things, depending on whether the object in question is singular or plural.
So our sentence above becomes,

- The child loves her. ¬ **Omwaana na-a-mu-kunda.** This is not to be confused with the following, which it resembles.

I like the child. ¬ **Omwaana na-mu-kunda!** ¬ Literally, The Child, I have liked it.

Example 3

SINGULAR

- **Omuntu ni-mu-kunda.**
- **Omuntu n-o-mu-kunda.**
- **Omuntu n-a-mu-kunda.**
- **Omuntu ni-tu-mu-kunda.**

PLURAL

- **Abantu nim-ba-kunda.**
- **Abantu n-o-ba-kunda.**
- **Abantu n-a-ba-kunda.**
- **Abantu ni-tu-ba-kunda.**

- **Omuntu ni-mu-mu-kunda.**
- **Abantu ni-mu-bakunda.**
  ¬ The first **mu** refers to *you* (plural). The second **mu** refers to "him" or "her". It is sheer coincidence that **"-mu-"** is the midfix for *you* but that also the same word forms the object pronoun that stands for "*him*" or "*her*".
- **Omuntu ni-ba-mu-kunda.**
- **Abantu ni-ba-ba-kunda.**
- **Ekitabo ni-n-ki-shoma.**
- **Ebitabo ni-mbi-shoma.**
- **Ekitabo n-o-ki-shoma.**
- **Ebitabo n-o-bi-shoma.**
- **Ekitabo n-a-ki-shoma.**
- **Ebitabo n-a-bi-shoma.**
- **Ekitabo ni-mu-ki-shoma.**
- **Ebitabo ni-mu-bi-shoma.**
- **Ekitabo ni-tu-ki-shoma.**
- **Ebitabo ni-tu-bi-shoma.**
- **Embwa no-gi-tuunga**
- **Embwa no-zi-tuunga**

ADDITIONAL OBJECT PRONOUNS

There are other object pronouns. These employ the preposition "with", which, in Lunyankole Lukiga, derives from "and". In other words, we indicate "in the company of" with the short, simple "and". So, "I saw Jack with Jill" is equivalent to "I saw Jack and Jill". Or, **Nkareeba Jack na Jill.**

A special object pronoun exists that places this form of "and" in front of pronominal indicators. These then help us to say, "with me", "with you", "with her" (or "with him"), "with us", "with you" (plural *you*), and "with them".

LUNYANKOLE-LUKIGA	ENGLISH
Naanye	With me
Naiwe	With you
Nawe	With him/with her

Naitwe	With us
Naimwe	With you (plural *you*)
Nabo	With them

It is important to remember that in Lunyankole-Lukiga nouns belong to different noun groups. The above object pronouns are, obviously, used when referring to people only. The pronouns given below are used where objects or things are involved. However, each object pronoun indicated here depends on the noun group to which a noun belongs.

In addition, we have, in Lunyankole-Lukiga, a penchant for using diminutive or derogatory references with respect to object-nouns. On occasion, we apply these to people as well. So, a little object can be referred to using the indicator **-ko-,** which means it is ridiculously small or insignificant. Or, an object can be so big or inflated that we may use the indicator, **-kyo-,** or **-rwo-,** in an unflattering way.

I have left the following object pronouns unexplained to urge you, the reader, to invite a Munyankole-Mukiga to explain them to you. Who knows, the exercise may help to start a new friendship.

- **Nakyo**
- **Nako**
- **Narwo**
- **Natwo**
- **Nagwo**
- **Nabyo**

Lightning Source UK Ltd.
Milton Keynes UK
176696UK00001B/49/P